Preventing Self-injury and Suicide in Women's Prisons

ISBN 978-1-909976-29-0 (Paperback)
ISBN 978-1-910979-04-4 (EPUB ebook)
ISBN 978-1-910979-05-1 (PDF ebook)

Cover design © 2016 Waterside Press.

Main UK distributor Gardners Books, 1 Whittle Drive, Eastbourne, East Sussex, BN23 6QH. Tel: +44 (0)1323 521777; sales@gardners.com; www.gardners.com

North American distribution Ingram Book Company, One Ingram Blvd, La Vergne, TN 37086, USA. Tel: (+1) 615 793 5000; inquiry@ingramcontent.com

Cataloguing-In-Publication Data A catalogue record for this book can be obtained from the British Library.

Printed by CPI Group, Chippenham, UK.

e-book *Preventing Self-injury and Suicide in Women's Prisons* is available as an ebook and also to subscribers of Myilibrary, Dawsonera, ebrary, and Ebscohost.

Published 2016 by
Waterside Press
Sherfield Gables
Sherfield-on-Loddon
Hook, Hampshire
United Kingdom RG27 0JG

Telephone +44(0)1256 882250
E-mail enquiries@watersidepress.co.uk
Online catalogue WatersidePress.co.uk

Preventing Self-injury and Suicide in Women's Prisons

Tammi Walker and Graham Towl

Foreword Lord Toby Harris

✦ WATERSIDE PRESS

'Walker and Towl's new book is a really welcome addition to the suicide and self-injury literature. It covers considerable ground in a concise and accessible way. Not only does it provide great coverage of the key issues around suicide and self-injury in women's prisons, it provides really helpful tips on supporting women, on staff training and on managing the aftermath of a suicide. I highly recommend this book':

Professor Rory O'Connor, University of Glasgow.

'Very helpful in identifying the strengths and weaknesses of current practice and understanding why reductions in the prison population and a holistic approach to care are vital in saving lives':

Dr Jo Borrill, University of Westminster.

'The question that arises from this book is, "How can we as a society heap any more punishment on people who are already punishing themselves?"':

Mark Johnson MBE, author of *Wasted* (Sphere, 2008), founder of the charity User Voice and CanDo Coffee.

'[The authors] bring an often neglected subject into sharp relief and, refreshingly, they are not afraid to make some strong, evidence-based assertions about the direction of penal policy and gaps in our understanding':

Anita Dockley, Research Director, Howard League for Penal Reform.

We dedicate this book to all the women and girls who have been imprisoned, we believe that you deserve to be treated with respect and enabled to achieve all that life has to offer.

A Personal Account from Tracey

'I started self-harming when I was ten-years-old, that was when the problems with my Mum started and I often ran away from home for periods of time, but when I was at home I self-harmed by cutting.

Self-harming made me feel relieved and it distracted me from the way I was feeling. At the time I was feeling really scared and puzzled about what was going to happen with my Mum and me. I still self-harm now that I am in prison, to cope you know, but I don't want to feel this way anymore or keep hurting myself. I want things to change.'

Table of Contents

3   Self-injury and Suicide Among Imprisoned Women and Adolescent Girls 45

4   Supporting Women and Adolescent Girls with Poly-victimisation Histories in Custody   63

5   Preventing Self-injury and Suicide   81

6   Staff Training for Self-injury and Suicide   101

Foreword

Lord Toby Harris

When my colleagues and I began our independent inquiry into the self-inflicted deaths of young people in prison or young offender institutions (YOIs) ('The Harris Review: Changing Prisons, Saving Lives', Cm 9087, July 2015), it was immediately apparent that virtually all of the tragic and avoidable deaths that we were examining were of boys and young men. Indeed of the 87 cases we examined in detail, only two were of young women. The received wisdom was that while women and young girls were more likely to self-harm, the number of self-inflicted deaths was greater amongst men and boys (although the absolute numbers in the male estate is far higher). Inevitably, therefore our focus was on the latter and therefore this book is important in that it goes some way to redressing the balance.

Tammi Walker and Graham Towl have identified over 100 women and adolescent girls who have taken their own lives in prison. Significantly, their wider review of more than 2,000 cases finds that patterns of suicidality are different for women and men. For example, the risk of suicide rises with age amongst men, but decreases amongst women. The danger is that the fact that there are so many more men in prison than there are women and that the absolute number of male suicides is so much greater will mask these different patterns. Any consideration of an overall average will mean that the male pattern will prevail, and issues specific to women and adolescent girls will be lost.

But it is too easy to get lost in the statistics. Every one of the self-inflicted deaths identified in this book or that we considered in our inquiry was someone's son or daughter, sister or brother, partner or even parent. What is more each self-inflicted death in prison represents a failure by the State to protect the prisoners concerned; each is a failure to comply with Article 2 of the European Convention On Human Rights.

The failure of the State is all the greater because in our work it was apparent that the same criticisms of prison regimes, systems and protocols had been repeated time and time again. Lessons had not been learned and not enough had been done to bring about substantive change.

One cannot help but feel that this is because as a society we value the lives of those in custody less than those at liberty. We need to recover what Winston Churchill, as Home Secretary (and therefore then responsible for the prison system), described in the House of Commons in 1910 as 'an unfaltering faith that there is a treasure, if only you can find it, in the heart of every man'. His reference to 'every man' reflects, of course, the mores of the early years of the last century, but it is also a reminder of the frequent invisibility of women in our penal system — then as now.

Addressing these problems is, of course, made harder because there are so many myths about prison nurtured in the media, that persist in describing incarceration as being more like attending a holiday camp than a punishment. In reality, prisons and YOIs are grim environments, bleak and demoralising to the spirit.

When you couple that with a recognition, as our inquiry found, that most young adults in custody are vulnerable, the experience of being in prison is particularly damaging to a developing young person.

Many prisoners have had chaotic lives and complex histories; some have been subjected to child abuse or exposed to violence; many have been in foster or residential care; and this background is often further compounded by mental health issues or a lack of maturity.

Our findings were that prisoners are not sufficiently engaged in purposeful activity and time is not spent in a constructive and valuable way. Current operational staffing levels are not adequate and the resultant restricted regimes do not even allow for the delivery of planned core day activities that might help rehabilitation.

Even more damaging is that with present staffing it is virtually impossible to focus on the individual prisoner. There is no one person who takes responsibility for the continuing safety or welfare of the individual prisoner. There is nobody to make sure that individual needs for education or training are met, or that the requirements for health and mental health care are adequately addressed. It is not surprising therefore that so few prisoners are successfully rehabilitated back into society at the end of a prison term.

Women face a number of additional particular needs in prison. They are often separated from children and this brings its own unique stress. Evidence that our inquiry received suggested that they have higher rates of trauma, victimisation, substance abuse and mental health issues.

Addressing their needs (and indeed those of all prisoners), ensuring their safety and enabling their rehabilitation requires clear leadership — from Ministers, senior officials in the Prison Service as well as those responsible for individual establishments. There needs to be a new philosophy underpinning our penal system — one which recognises that a primary purpose of prison is the rehabilitation of prisoners and that requires that all prisoners are valued and nurtured towards safer, more productive lives.

Each prisoner needs to be treated as an individual with a personal plan to bring about that rehabilitation by addressing their individual needs and a suitably trained and empathetic officer needs to take personal responsibility for ensuring that that plan is delivered.

Better still, of course, is to address those needs long before the prisoner ends up in custody. In many of the 87 cases we examined, the problems and vulnerabilities, including their mental health issues, of the young people had been evident from an early age. The question we posed is 'Why did so many of them end up in custody?'.

Far more needs to be done to divert young people away from the criminal justice system. Cross-governmental input is needed to address the multi-faceted problems that troubled children and adolescents face, but tackling those issues early is likely to save the State the costs of their future criminal behaviour and potentially their imprisonment. And, if fewer people end up in prison, then resources can be focused on those that do end up there to ensure that they are not only safe and secure but that the individual support they need can be available.

My hope is that our inquiry will spur a change in political attitudes to prison and the policy approach to criminal justice. And that this excellent book will ensure that the different experiences, vulnerabilities and needs of women and adolescent girls are properly taken into account.

Lord Toby Harris
September 2015

About the authors

Tammi Walker has worked in forensic settings for over 15 years, engaging directly with individuals who are a risk to themselves and others and, in a consultancy rôle, with teams and services that care for and manage them. She is a member of the Advisory Group for the Suicide Prevention in Prisons initiative being delivered by the Howard League for Penal Reform and the Centre for Mental Health and a member of the Oversight Group for the Women's Rivendell Service at HM Prison New Hall. She has research interests in the areas of women, self-injury, suicide, trauma and resilience in staff, all of which she has published on. Currently she is leading a project that is examining the nature and extent of all recorded deaths in state custody in England and Wales from 2000 to 2014. She is Principal Lecturer in Psychology at Manchester Metropolitan University, a Chartered Psychologist and Associate Fellow registered with the British Psychological Society.

Graham Towl is a leading expert on suicide in prisons. He is a member of the Independent Advisory Panel on Deaths in Custody and was a member of the Harris Review into Self Inflicted Deaths (SIDs) of 18 to 24-year-olds in Prisons. Currently he is writing up research into the SIDs of over 2,000 prisoners from 1978 to 2014. He is uniquely the recipient of British Psychological Society Awards for Distinguished Contributions to both Professional Practice and Forensic Academic Knowledge. He has worked as a practitioner, policy-maker and researcher in this challenging field. He is the co-editor (with David Crighton) of the British Psychological Society endorsed postgraduate textbook *Forensic Psychology* (Wiley-Blackwell, 2010; 2015). Graham Towl is Professor of Forensic Psychology and Pro-Vice-Chancellor and Deputy Warden at Durham University. Formerly he was Chief Psychologist at the United Kingdom's Ministry of Justice.

The author of the Foreword

Lord Toby Harris was Chair of the Independent Advisory Panel on Deaths in Custody from 2009 to 2015. In February 2014, he was asked by the Minister for Prisons to lead the review into self-inflicted deaths in National Offender Management Service (NOMS) custody. This was completed in April 2015, published in July 2015, and made recommendations to reduce the risk of such deaths.

Acknowledgements

We would like to acknowledge all of the women and adolescent girls we have worked with professionally over the years and say thank you to them for the insight and understanding gained from that experience.

We would also like to acknowledge and thank the Waterside Press editorial team, in particular Bryan for the editing, guidance, and feedback on the drafts and endless emails we have sent.

CHAPTER 1

Suicide and Self-injury of Imprisoned Women and Adolescent Girls

Introduction

This book is about imprisoned women and adolescent girls who have completed suicide and/or injured themselves. In 2011 the self-inflicted death (SID) of the 100th recorded imprisoned woman to kill herself in an English jail (there are currently no prisons for women in Wales) took place. This landmark was reached, went largely unnoticed and subsequently passed (Towl, 2015).

We do not know how many women or men killed themselves in our prisons prior to 1978 because in England and Wales this was not systematically recorded and no case level records were kept, however, we would anticipate that there had been suicides by prisoners. This is perhaps one powerful indication of the very low level of historic concern for prisoners taking their own lives. This is an important historic context. Politics, policies, research and practices have moved on and we trace some of these key developments below. We have chosen to focus upon women and adolescent girls because such cases can tend to get hidden amid generalisations about suicidal prisoners. One of the most recent lessons in suicide research is that prevention strategies need to target a range of sub-groups with differing needs. This will be the key to any future successful strategies for reducing the numbers of SIDs amongst both women and men. There are many different motivations for suicide. Suicide can involve a range of different activities albeit all resulting in death.

Elsewhere we have previously argued that the politics of the day are more impactful in informing policy and practice than research (Towl and Walker, 2015). This is the case in prisons as much as it is elsewhere in public services. However, it can remain a popular fiction that policy development in criminal justice is evidence based. At best we believe it to be evidence informed.

In this short chapter we cover key themes, which, we think have significant importance in our understanding of the topic.

Suicide and Self-injury

In a recent Ministry of Justice (MoJ) statistical bulletin based upon research undertaken by MoJ analysts and Graham Towl on SIDs in prison custody in England and Wales between January 1978 and March 2014 there were 2,014 such deaths recorded, 103 of who were women and adolescent girls (Ministry of Justice, Statistical Notice, 2015). Broadly, women and adolescent girls have historically made up to around five per cent of the prisoner population (Ministry of Justice, 2015b). Detailed studies have indicated that overall women and adolescent girls have had a slightly lower rate of suicide in prisons than men (Crighton, 2000). Of course such historical patterns may change over time. Calculating rates based on statistically small numbers can be unreliable so we do need to view the figures with some caution. Also it is important to be cognisant of the need to compare both across and within related community-based population rates. In other words, it is important to not only compare the rates of suicide between imprisoned women and adolescent girls and men and adolescent boys but also the ratio of such suicides across the genders in the community too. But wherever and however such comparisons are completed our central concern is with reducing the actual number of suicides in prisons. We have a similar aim in relation to both the rates and absolute number of occurrences of self-injury in prisons too, i.e. a reduction of the numbers of avoidable such deaths.

As we shall cover in the chapters that follow, the reasons for suicide and self-injury in prisons are multifactorial (Task Force on Suicide, 1994; McHugh and Snow, 2000; WHO, 2007; Walker, 2015). There are three key general reasons why we are focusing upon prisoner suicide. First, there is the loss of life by a potentially avoidable death, second, those who come from socially and economically disadvantaged groups with high levels of need are over-represented in prisoner populations and thirdly they are under the care of the State (Towl and Walker, 2015). The care in State care needs to mean something more meaningful. We have two specific additional reasons for a focus upon women and adolescent girls. First, imprisoned women and adolescent girls are in a minority with often different needs and concerns to those of imprisoned men and adolescent boys. Second the rates of self-injury in particular are higher in women and adolescent girls and as we describe in subsequent chapters this can be the product of their, often abusive, childhoods and sometimes adulthoods.

New Punitiveness and Managerialism

The prisoner population in England and Wales has increased more than twofold since the 1990s (Ministry of Justice, 2015). Our best prediction is that as prisoner populations continue to increase so will prisoner suicides in the absence of more robust approaches to suicide prevention. But even if governments and courts continue to grow their prisoner populations, much can still be done to reduce the rates of suicide.

The new punitiveness has impacted upon not only the absolute numbers of prisoners but also in the characterisation of prisoners as offenders with a collection of 'criminogenic needs' in need of 'treatment' with (experimental) programmes. The idea is that prisoners have some faulty thinking and this needs correction. A number of 'correctional services' have attempted to address such issues through comparatively largescale programmes. The aims of such programmes have been asserted to be the reduction of reoffending (House of Commons Research Paper, 2012). This is sometimes measured with psychometric tests and sometimes with reconviction rates (House of Commons Research Paper, 2012). Putting aside the precept that we can 'target' such 'criminogenic factors' which seems more a product of hope than reason, clearly a holistic understanding of prisoners and their unique needs was an early casualty of such approaches.

In addition to the new punitiveness briefly outlined above there has been a growing managerialist conceptualisation of running public services. This has led to a need for further measurement, particularly of what is viewed as 'performance'. So, in the managerialist lexicon there are key performance indicators (KPIs) such as the number of 'completions' on 'programmes' (NOMS, 2014). Such broad targets serve to create perverse incentives. For example, prisoners being put on courses where there is unlikely to be benefit, or being required to inappropriately repeat such courses. The courses themselves are often based on experimental approaches and there are insufficient such courses to meet the apparent referral need. It is not hard to see how the individual prisoner is easily forgotten in all this managerial malaise.

But the key point in relation to our understanding of suicide and self-injury is not that many of the frustrations resulting from such new punitiveness and managerialism may drive individuals to further despair, although we would not rule that out. The point is that the danger of the individual needs of prisoners will be unseen and instead only 'criminogenic need' focused upon or 'targeted' as such treatment industry advocates would have it.

We would conclude that one impact of the treatment industry in prisons has been to put into the background the mental health needs of prisoners and this is perhaps especially so for women and adolescent girls in view of their lack of visibility when compared with men and adolescent boys in the prison system and also their, on average, higher needs for support in view of their particular backgrounds prior to imprisonment.

Mental Health Needs

The most major, yet often forgotten and unmet mental health need for imprisoned women and adolescent girls and men and adolescent boys, is their need to adapt to the transition into a new environment. This mental health challenge is by far the most single significant mental health consideration with suicidal prisoners. And indeed it is unsurprising that the risk of suicide is appreciably higher at the early stages of imprisonment (Crighton and Towl, 1997; Towl and Crighton, 1998; Shaw *et al*, 2004). So-called psychiatric morbidity studies reflect psychiatric models of mental illness and not the everyday mental health challenges that are linked to an increased risk of suicide. Thus they are restricted to psychiatrically defined categories of mental distress or difficulty thereby excluding the more plausibly germane unmet mental health need of positive adaptation to a new and coercive environment such as a prison.

This is not to suggest that psychiatric diagnostic categories are irrelevant to suicide risk, but rather that they are limited, sometimes overstated and generally of comparatively little utility in terms of reducing the risk of suicide in prisons because as categories they do not discriminate well between those who do go on to kill themselves and those who do not. Also in some of the chapters that follow the often circular nature of some diagnostic categories is touched upon, for example with what is termed 'borderline personality disorder' (BPD) where evidence of self-injury may contribute to such a diagnosis. So, it is not clear if what is proposed is that those who 'have' BPD are more likely to self-injure, or if those who self-injure are more likely to develop BPD. We think that such terms take us little further forward in helping those who are suicidal or self-injuring. One way of testing the utility of such terminology is to ask who benefits from its use. It does not seem to be imprisoned women and adolescent girls who do, far from it.

The international evidence remains firmly supportive of the assertion that the transition from a more familiar environment to the unfamiliar environment of a particular prison is a time of heightened risk of suicide (WHO, 2007). Prison Service policy has to some degree reflected this need as we shall see in the chapters ahead. For example, by investing in support for prisoners especially during the early days of their arrival in prisons (Grubin *et al*, 2003; Hall and Gabor, 2004; Dockley, 2008) hence the significant investment in local prisons earlier this century by HM Prison Service which was evidence informed and a largely successful development.

Themes and Perspectives: Language

Language is important, nowhere more so than with imprisoned women and adolescent girls who are suicidal and or self-injuring. One of the regrettable themes in this area of research, policy and practice is the frequent use amongst many of pejorative language to refer to those who are suicidal or self-injuring (Dear *et al*, 2001; Short *et al*, 2009). Such rituals are at odds with guidance for ethical and professional practice across healthcare professionals (Health and Care Professions Council, 2008). They are also at odds with the espoused organizational values of the Prison Service. But critically such a demeaning and disrespectful approach may well serve to increase the chances of there being yet more avoidable SIDs. For example, if imprisoned women and adolescent girls hear how those with suicidal ideas of self-injurious behaviour are talked about in a pejorative fashion they may be less likely to come forward with the expression of suicidal ideation or indeed they may self-injure covertly. But arguably most importantly any such pejorative language is a potential additional barrier to the enactment of therapeutic change. Given the high level of challenge of working effectively with suicidal and self-injurious imprisoned women and adolescent girls we think it imperative that staff challenge colleagues using pejorative language which has no place in research, policy or practice. Subsequent chapters in this book detail some of the pejorative language sometimes used. But to give the reader a flavour we are thinking of references to dismissing behaviour as 'attention seeking' and so on (Dear *et al*, 2001; Short *et al*, 2009). It is axiomatic that prison managers need to challenge such practices in their prisons whether or not it is linked to suicide and self-injury.

Themes and Perspectives: Criminal Justice Ideology

Mental health needs of prisoners are rarely the top priority in the criminal justice process. Indeed the focus is largely and (and understandably) routinely on containment and reducing the risk of reconviction. Both these aims are seen to contribute to public protection. The danger is that the members of the public not protected are the imprisoned women, men and children. This tension is reflected in a number of ways with e.g. adolescent girls being referred to as 'juveniles' giving their criminal justice status primacy over their needs as a child. We have consciously used the term imprisoned 'women and adolescent girls' throughout to reflect a more holistic understanding of the person and their needs rather than writing simply in terms of the 'female estate' or 'females', as one

Prison Service colleague once commented this could be taken to include goldfish! If we are to help women and adolescent girls at a potentially vulnerable time and place in their lives then a prerequisite is surely compassion and an ability to see and try and understand the whole person.

Whereas it has often been observed that there are inherent tensions between 'care' and 'control' they are not mutually exclusive concepts (Towl and Fisher, 1990). Showing care and compassion does not mean neglecting issues of security. Nor does exercising control have to mean showing a lack of respect for prisoners.

The chapters ahead cover what we consider to be some of the key issues in relation to suicide and self-injury in prisons in general but with a particular resonance and relevance for imprisoned women and adolescent girls.

We begin with a general coverage of suicide and self-injury in prisons and follow this with a chapter focused upon women and adolescent girls in particular. Much of the research simply refers to studies of suicides either explicitly excluding women or not mentioning their presence in the overall figures. We noted above that a significant part of the future, if we are to strive to be evidence informed in our policies and practices, will be a focus on the needs of clearly defined and differing groups rather than presuming an implicit one size fits all approach. *Chapter 4* of this book includes an exploration and explication of the importance of us having a greater understanding of poly-victimisation histories (Finkelhor *et al*, 2005) and the resultant traumas that we need to be mindful of when working with our clients. The fundamental importance of ensuring that any of our interventions or interactions with such clients is trauma informed (Hannah-Moffatt, 2010; Covington, 2014) cannot be overemphasised in our view.

Chapter 5 is about prevention. We think that prevention is more important than prediction in research, policy and practice. We take a public health based approach with a layering of responses dependent upon likely need. For example, we emphasise the importance of retaining the injection of significant structure and resources at the earliest stages of incarceration. That is the case for everyone. But then as staff get to know prisoners more there may well be opportunities to tailor responses accordingly. Once an individual reports suicidal thoughts or feelings there would then need to be another such level of assessment and intervention.

If one of three main messages from this book is taken forward by those resourced to do so, it would be the need for staff training being on a mandatory footing that we would advocate primarily for the benefit of prisoners but also for the benefit of the staff themselves to ensure that they are confident and knowledgeable in working in such a challenging area.

The second call in this book, put simply, is for government and the courts to cut the number of people that we are imprisoning as a country. As mentioned elsewhere the prisoner population including women has doubled over the past 20 years or so and it is not clear that budgets have been increased in line with that increase, indeed what is clear is that prison officer numbers are on the decrease (Howard League, 2014).

Our third, and key call, is to recognise that although women may have some commonalities with men in terms of their needs there are differences and sometimes significant differences too and this book is hopefully a reminder of the need for us to ensure that we shape services according to meet the considerable unmet needs of imprisoned women and adolescent girls.

Chapter Summary Points

- The major mental health need of imprisoned women and adolescent girls is systematically missed from psychiatric morbidity studies. The often unmet mental health need in question is the adaptation to an unfamiliar environment, namely imprisonment.

- We imprison too many women and criminal justice policy and practice has primacy in prisons and this sometimes gives rise to tensions between the needs of the criminal justice process and the wellbeing of prisoners.

- Staff need high quality (mandatory) training to support them in the

challenging rôles of working with suicidal and self-injuring imprisoned women and adolescent girls.

Future Directions

It is early in the term of the current government in England and Wales but if imprisonment numbers continue to rise so, we would anticipate, will suicide numbers. Whatever the political flavour of the government may be there is a need to ensure that we apply the research that we have rather than simply fund yet further research. This is especially important against a backdrop of public sector cuts. Future improvements need to be evidence informed and there remains much data for us to draw upon to make positive changes and reduce the number and rate of imprisoned women and adolescent girls tragically taking their own lives.

CHAPTER 2

Self-injury and Suicide: Research Informed Change

Overview

In this chapter we begin with a discussion exploring and examining the definitional and contextual issues associated with suicide and self-injury. We will highlight some of the differing definitions and terminology used in this area, both in research and practice. Next we review the development of policy and practice in self-injury and suicide risk prevention in prisons. Particular attention is given to the last 20 years, during which a range of guidance and instructional documents have been developed and distributed. We conclude with a consideration of some of the problems and challenges of the implementation of research informed change.

Definitional Issues

Terms such as self-injury, attempted suicide and suicide in prison warrant clear definition. Until 1961 suicide was a crime in England and Wales and legal definitions of suicide today remain grounded largely in criminal law. For example, it is generally said that an individual has 'committed' suicide rather than using the more impartial or neutral and increasingly widely used description of 'completed' suicide (Crighton and Towl, 2008). In a coroner's court, if the verdict of suicide is reached this requires the criminal burden of proof, i.e. being proven beyond all reasonable doubt. It is acknowledged that official statistics give an underestimate of the true prevalence of suicide, with many such self-inflicted deaths (SIDs) being documented as due to an accident, misadventure, open verdicts or unknown causes. The official figures on the estimates of the rates of suicide are therefore likely to be inaccurate and underesti-mate the actual number of individuals who end their own lives (Jenkins and Singh, 2000). Epidemiological studies that apply the International Classification of Diseases (ICD) categories provide more detailed, com-prehensive and internationally comparable baselines than legally defined suicide rates (Crighton, 2012). This does mean that we need to be cau-tious when comparing, for example, rates of suicide amongst prisoners and the general population. Official figures on prisoner suicide give the number for SIDs, which will be higher than that for those with a ver-dict simply of suicide.

Defining self-injury and attempted suicide in England and Wales are equally as complex, and legal systems have sought to move away from defining them. With regard to the legal framework, definitions of such behaviour have largely been limited to mainly tangential areas (Crighton, 2012) as in, for example, the Mental Health Acts or the Female Genital Mutilation Act 2011. Arguably a key challenge here is the point at which self-injury or self-poisoning may be defined as attempted suicide, and, also whether there are any clear cut-offs within what is sometimes con-ceptualised as the continuum from mild to severe self-injury (Crighton, 2012). In the United Kingdom the concept of 'Deliberate Self-Harm' (Morgan, 1979) became extensively used from the early-1980s, however the notion of 'self-harm' is problematic. Firstly, it is very broad, includ-ing self-cutting, self-poisoning, drug use, excessive eating, tattooing and piercing (Walsh and Rosen, 1988). In an attempt to pragmatically address this issue, a definitional approach was put forward that did not include the less severe forms of self-injury and this approach has largely been used in practice in the United Kingdom (Pattison and Kahan, 1983). Some have argued there is little logical basis for this approach (Walsh and Rosen, 1988; Towl, 1997; Crighton, 2012). Secondly, the notion of 'delib-erate' in self-injurious behaviours has been questioned and challenged (Towl, 2000; Crighton and Towl, 2002; Crighton, 2012). The func-tion and amount of deliberation is often unclear or sometimes entirely absent (Crighton, 2012). For some the term 'deliberate' has a pejora-tive tone to it. In order to address this issue a more specific, alternative term such as 'intentional self-injury' has been proposed as it does not have expectations about the amount of associated thought and planning (Towl *et al,* 2002). However, such terminology has gained little ground in practice (Crighton, 2012). Indeed, we would argue that simply using the term self-injury may be best in terms of semantic parsimony and, in particular, not making motivational inferences.

Separating attempted suicide from the notions of self-injury and self-poisoning has its challenges as practitioners and researchers often viewed them as being interrelated behaviours. However, this view was questioned, and the term 'para-suicide' was put forward (Kreitman, 1977) to refer to a full range of acts where there appeared to be an absence of intention to die. Such definitions became popular in the 1970s and 1980s but it has been suggested that perhaps more difficulties were raised than solved. For example, even though there are many incidents where those who engage in self-injury have no intention to die, it is open to question how far this may be generalised (Towl and Crighton, 2002). Other terms such as *self-mutilative behaviours* (Nock and Prinstein, 2004), *self-mutilation* (Favazza, 1998), *deliberate self-harm* (Pattison and Kahan, 1983), and *non-suicidal self-injury* (Muehlenkamp, 2006) have been used to refer to direct and deliberate tissue damage, inflicted without conscious intent to die. Several of these definitions have been used to explain self-injury that is demonstrated by individuals with learning disabilities, or in response to mental health related delusions (Jeglic, Vanderhoff and Donovick, 2005).

Intent issues in completed suicides are often unclear, with confused and mixed intentions typically seen in both completed and attempted suicides and those who self-injure (Shneidman, 1985; Crighton 2006; Crighton, 2012). There is considerable overlap between those groups who engage in self-injury and those who attempt suicide, and it is important to understand how they differ too. The intent to die is critical to assess in such cases, individuals may report having an ambivalence concerning their level of intent to die (Brown, Comtois and Linehan, 2002). Individuals who attempt suicide often present with very different behavioural presentations and histories than those who engage in self-injury (Fulwiler *et al*, 1997). For example, it was found that prisoners who engaged in self-injury described more impulsivity, while those with a history of suicidal behaviours stated more depressive symptoms (Lohner and Konrad,

2006). Additionally, although self-injury is correlated with suicidality, a very significant number of individuals with a history of self-injury never attempt suicide (Dulit, Fyer, Leon, Brodsky and Frances, 1994; Schwartz, Cohen, Hoffman and Meeks, 1989). Lastly, the purpose of suicide is different from that of self-injury. The aim of suicide is to end life, while many scholars conceptualise self-injury as functioning to often support individuals to adapt to life; it acts as a form of *self-preservation* (Walker *et al*, 2015, Gratz, 2003; Pattison and Kahan, 1983).

Definitional concerns in prison-based studies

Terminology and definitions used in prison-based studies have had similar issues as community studies, particularly in self-injury research. Clear differences do emerge in relation to prison-based research studies. For example, a large number of community studies have described a prevalence of self-poisoning, however, in distinct contrast; prison samples have reported lower incidences of self-poisoning. In a recent review of self-injury in prisoner populations it was found that cutting and scratching were the most frequent self-injurious methods in both sexes (Hawton *et al*, 2013); in imprisoned women and adolescent girls, self-strangulation was common (31% of all episodes) followed by hanging (Crighton and Towl, 2002; Liebling and Krarup, 1993; Howard League, 2003). Most incidents of self-injury in prisons have been reported as being of low lethality, particularly in imprisoned women and adolescent girls (Hawton *et al*, 2013). It therefore remains unclear, how comparable the results of community studies and prison-based studies are, and how far the findings of community-based studies may be used to advise and inform research and practice in forensic institutions. We may conclude that we need caution with any such comparisons.

Issues of reporting and exposure of incidents additionally complicate studies undertaken in forensic settings. In research undertaken in the community, for the most part, service users who self-present for treatment at Accident and Emergency Departments are focused upon (Harricks *et al*, 2003; Kapur *et al*, 1998). Research has indicated that there is an increased possibility that a significant number of incidents of self-injury are 'hidden' in the community due to under-reporting (Kapur *et al*, 1998).

Individuals in the community are more likely to self-treat their wounds, with the possible exclusion of individuals who have self-poisoned. In stark contrast, incidents of self-injury in prison may be more likely to be reported (Crighton and Towl, 2002). Within this book, for expository purposes, we use the term self-injury to refer to, '*any act where a prisoner deliberately harms themselves irrespective of the method, intent or severity of any injury.*' (Ministry of Justice, 2013b, p.14).

Contextual Issues Associated with Self-injury and Suicide

Suicide is a complex phenomenon and a serious public health problem for individuals in prison or elsewhere. Custodial settings differ internationally with respect to prisoner populations and local arrangements to identify, monitor and manage self-injurious and suicidal behaviour (Humber *et al*, 2011). Prison Service prevention strategies in England and Wales for self-injury and suicide have often sought to identify or 'find' the solution to this problem. However, there is a singular range of factors and motivations prompted by differing circumstances as to *why* individuals injure themselves. Strategies for prevention that have been developed in prisons have attempted to take account of factors external and internal to the prison and the individual prisoner as causative of self-injury/suicidal behaviour (McHugh and Snow, 2000). However, a major problem facing policy makers in developing and initiating prevention in prisons is simply the range of factors that may possibly impact upon individual self-injury and suicide risk. By way of illustration, each of the following common prison factors have been proposed as influencing the degree of risk:

Individual factors
- being from a white ethnic grouping (Abel *et al*, 2015; World Health Organization (WHO, 2007);
- being relatively young (WHO, 2007) or older if men and younger if women (Harris Review, 2015);
- having a history of previous self-injury (Abel *et al*, 2015; WHO, 2007);

- coming from disadvantaged social, economic and familial back-grounds, (Abel *et al*, 2015; WHO, 2007);
- serving longer sentences (Dear, Thomson, Howells, and Hall, 2001);
- having a history of disciplinary violations (Dear, Thomson, Howells, and Hall, 2001);
- having experienced or witnessed some form of emotional, physical and/sexual abuse (Abel *et al*, 2015; WHO, 2007);a history of psychiatric disorder and treatment (Abel *et al*, 2015; WHO, 2007);
- having a past of alcohol and/or drug dependency (Abel *et al*, 2015; WHO, 2007);
- being convicted of sexual and violent offences (Dear, Thomson, Howells, and Hall, 2001).

Situational factors
- the extent to which prisoners have availability of potential liga-tures and ligature points (Ministry of Justice, 2011);
- the degree to which staffing levels are low (Liebling, 2006; Prisons and Probation Ombudsman, 2011);
- the extent of housing accommodation available to prisoners such as single celled (Metzner and Hayes, 2006);
- the extent of overcrowding in prisons (Crighton, 2000; Howard League, 2005).

Psychosocial factors
- the extent to which prisoners are able to maintain social and family ties (WHO, 2007);
- the availability for prisoners to gain access to services to support mental health and emotional difficulties (WHO, 2007);
- the extent to which prisoners feel safe and protected from bullying (Prisons and Probation Ombudsman, 2011; WHO, 2007);
- the extent to which prisoners have routes and opportunities to disclose and discuss problems (WHO, 2007).

These lists are by no means exhaustive, but they do (for successful prevention prison-based interventions ne coordinated to accommodate a range of potential situa cial and individual factors.

It has been argued that prison officers have to de sion between their custody and care rôles when responding to prisoners (Home Office, 1991; Towl and Forbes, 2002) which entails them balancing the needs of security with humanity. Conflict and ambiguity may occur within the rôles of prison staff (Triplett, Mullings and Scarborough, 1996) that may cause psychological strain and low job satisfaction (Cox, 1993; Mackay *et al*, 2004). Secondly, there is the effect of unintended or unforeseen consequences (McHugh and Snow, 2000). It must be highlighted that changes in Prison Service policies may impact upon self-injury and suicide risk in unintentional ways, for example, engaging prisoners in meaningful activity is a Prison Service objective, however, increased time in association may lead to an increase in occasions for prisoners being intimidated or bullied by others, unless supervision is satisfactory. This could then, in turn, lead to more indirect but positive outcomes with improved social contacts. An overview of how current Prison Service policy has developed follows.

Prison Service Monitoring and Management of Self-injury and Suicide Up Until 2000

In the 1970s and 1980s there was a growing political, public and media interest in the increasing problem of self-injury and SIDs in prisons (McHugh and Snow, 2000). For example, a Home Office (1984) report emphasised the importance of the rôle of medical officers in identifying suicidal prisoners and the need to improve medical regimes to identify and manage those prisoners who were deemed at high risk of suicide. As a result of this report there was introduced the Working Group on Suicide Prevention (1986) and this resulted in the publishing of instructions specifying medical assessment, support for prisoners, management of suicide prevention and the forming of suicide prevention management groups in all prisons (Speed, 2012). These proposals stressed the need to recognise the 'onset and development' of suicide rather than identifying a 'type' of prisoner who may commit suicide (McHugh and Snow, 2000).

Following on from these developments came the first full thematic review by Her Majesty's Chief Inspectorate of Prisons (*The Tumim Report*) in 1990 and this made 123 recommendations. A key aspect of this report was that it highlighted that Prison Service policy did not reflect the significance of the environment in which the prisoners and staff functioned. Thus the age-old psychological maxim that human behaviour always occurs in an environmental context was perhaps sometimes not taken account of. This report had major ramifications and there was a re-examination of the current approaches of suicide prevention. The Suicide Awareness Support Unit (SASU) was founded with the aim of supporting prisoners and ensuring good practice within the Prison Service.

In 1994, the Caring for the Suicidal in Custody strategy was introduced and there was a clearer focus on a more multi-disciplinary approach, which gave all staff the responsibility to identify and support suicidal prisoners. The F2052SH form (self-harm at-risk) was introduced and it could be 'triggered' by any member of staff who had concerns regarding a prisoner. The use of these forms was 'patchy' and it was often viewed as including poor individualised care planning, an absence of professional accountability and inadequate care plans (HM Inspectorate of Prisons, 1999; Royal College of Psychiatrists, 2002; Senior *et al*, 2002).

Also incorporated in this strategy was Prison Service policy on suicides, the rôle of Suicide Awareness Teams (SATs) and the rôle of the Samaritans and Listener schemes. Listeners are prisoners trained and supported by the Samaritans and they work to prevent self-injury and suicide by offering a confidential listening service (Hancock and Graham, 2008). In 1999 the *Suicide is Everyone's Concern* report involved a detailed review of prison suicide prevention procedures. A number of proposals were listed including refining the suicide strategy in local prisons and for women along with the need to improve Suicide Awareness Teams (HM Chief Inspectorate of Prisons for England and Wales, 1999).

Strategic Factors in the Year 2000 and Beyond

At the start of this period, suicide prevention in custody mainly focused on the identification and observation of prisoners at an inflated risk of suicide. This strategy had several significant flaws, for example, the difficulties in determining risk among already 'risky populations' and challenges of implementation (HM Chief Inspectorate of Prisons for England and Wales, 1999). Rising numbers of suicides, increasing criticism by reform organizations and management concern about the Caring for the Suicidal in Custody (1994) strategy led to it being replaced by Prison Service Order (PSO) 2700: Suicide and Self-harm Prevention, which began in 2003. Thus, the importance of 'prevention' over 'awareness' was re-stated and re-focused upon. The practice for caring for a prisoner at an inflated risk of self-injury and suicide was more clearly outlined, as were the precise rôles, duties and responsibilities of staff. Specific factors associated with increased suicidal risk, such as, the early stages of custody and drug withdrawal were also clearly identified.

From 2001 to 2004, the Prison Service set up an extensive programme called the Safer Custody Programme that consisted of major policy plans to develop and trial enhanced ways of reducing suicides. This incorporated a wide variety of initiatives, such as new systems of prisoner peer support, developments in reception screening and induction procedures, improved integration with healthcare, modified criteria for self-injury and suicides including environmental risk assessments, mental health in-reach, risk information transfer, deaths in custody investigations policy and detoxification units (Humber *et al,* 2011). The programme incorporated the appointment of full-time suicide prevention co-ordinators in local prisons, which were recognised as environments where there was a higher risk of suicide. This was an important development because it was a formal recognition of the need to shift away from an understanding of suicidality based chiefly on individual factors and take a more balanced evidence informed approach. The key purpose of the suicide prevention co-ordinator rôle was to ensure a high-quality level of support to prisoners at an inflated risk of suicide or self-injury through adherence to national and local policy, dissemination of good practice and promoting 'a safe and caring environment' (HM Prison Service, 2001).

The Prison Service completely revised the care planning system in this programme for at-risk prisoners and introduced Assessment, Care in Custody and Teamwork (ACCT) in 2004 although full implementation took a little longer. This system retained much of the philosophy of the F2052SH form with a multi-disciplinary approach. The ACCT has three levels and allows any member of staff to activate an ACCT plan. Once monitored under this system, the ACCT is said to be 'open' and following satisfactory reductions in the perceived risks, the prisoner is no longer observed and monitored under the system and the ACCT is then deemed 'closed'. The ACCT introduced safer cells (e.g. cells designed to reduce potential ligature points and types), which in theory reduced the chances of prisoners completing suicide, and ensured they were safe within their cells (HM Prison Service, 2007; Speed, 2012). However, the Safer Custody Programme has been criticised and it has been described as an 'oxymoron' as there has been little verification of evidence to demonstrate and establish that policies and procedures in place aimed to create a safe environment have worked (Goldson and Coles, 2005: xviii). Furthermore, others have critically commented upon the ACCT because of poor training and inconsistencies between what it intended to achieve and what it actually has (Rickford and Edgar, 2005).

The rôle of healthcare in the prison system has changed over the last two decades. Notwithstanding some fundamental problems with such comparisons, it has frequently been asserted that prisoners have been reported as having dramatically higher rates of a whole range of mental health problems including suicide and self-injury compared to the general population (Durcan, 2008). Others view an overreliance on diagnoses in the mental health field more generally as part of the problem distracting policy makers and practitioners from what may be viewed as psychosocial issues (e.g. Kinderman, 2014). Previously, prisoners identified as being at an inflated risk of harming themselves were often isolated in prison healthcare and it was possible that for those who repetitively self-injured that this may have made their situation worse (Howard League, 2001b). In 2001 the Department of Health introduced the principle of 'equivalence' into prison health care in England and Wales which meant that prisoners should receive the same quality of care for their health as they would receive outside prison (Royal College of Nursing, 2010). Some have argued that there is indeed equivalence of care across prisons and the community in that there remains what is sometimes referred to as a 'postcode lottery' with both such settings (Towl, 2010). New in-reach teams have been located in every prison in England (Royal College of Nursing, 2010). These teams were intended to be similar to Community Mental Health Teams (CMHT) that operate outside the prison system and incorporate within them the outreach and crisis resolution functions of the specialist teams that were developed across the United Kingdom with the publication of the *National Service Framework for Mental Health* (Department of Health, 1999). Evidence from a review (2010) that examined what had been achieved in prison mental health by the in-reach teams in England concluded that there had been improved responses to mental ill health among offenders, for example, through better screening on reception into prison, drug treatment and suicide prevention. However, specific reference of the impact of in-reach teams to responding to suicide and self-injuring prisoners was a notable omission from the review.

First night centres were introduced as another positive preventative measure in prisons to help ease the transition for those entering into custody as the historical and international evidence strongly indicates that the immediate aftermath of an individual's arrival at prison is a time of heightened risk of self-harm and suicide (Smith, 1984). A dedicated wing, or unit, where all new prisoners spend their first 48 hours at the prison can make a real contribution to saving lives. Such facilities are led by dedicated staff and include support and assistance from fellow prisoners. They are furnished in a less harsh way than normal prison accommodation and provide information and immediate contact with families and children. Their overall aim is to reduce the distress that many individuals feel at being sent to prison. Unfortunately there appear to be insufficient places in these first night centres according to some commentators (Howard League, 2005).

The Joint Committee on Human Rights published a report in 2004 on *Deaths in Custody* that advocated there was a need for a system to capture knowledge and ideas across sectors, following such deaths. From this, the independently chaired Forum for Preventing Deaths in Custody was established in 2006, which aimed to identify learning opportunities resulting from deaths across the numerous custodial settings, and preventing future deaths. In 2008, an independent review included criticism of the forum for its lack of authority and for being too large and diverse to be efficient as a decision-making organization (Ministry of Justice, 2008). Since 2009 the Ministerial Council on Deaths in Custody has been in operation, which is jointly funded by the Ministry of Justice, Department of Health and the Home Office. It comprises of three tiers, the first of which is a ministerial board, the second tier is the Independent Advisory Panel on Deaths in Custody (IAPDC), which is an advisory non-departmental public body. The IAPDC was chaired by Lord Toby Harris of Haringey from 2009 to 2015 and consisted of six independent expert panel members and they advised Ministers and the board on measures to reduce deaths in custody. Lastly, there is a broad-based stakeholder and practitioner group that consists of over 100 members, representing the interests of families, third sector organisations, practitioners from all sectors and the inspectorate and investigatory bodies. Further, since 2004, the Prisons and Probations Ombudsman (PPO) has investigated every death occurring in prisons, young offender institutions, probation-approved premises, and immigration removal centres (Shaw and Turnbull, 2009). When a failure of care has been identified, recommendations for improvements are made.

Evaluating the Changes

In England and Wales, there appears to have been an overall sustained reduction in the overall number of SIDs. Between 2005 and 2011, the number of SIDs per year generally declined, but in 2012 and 2013 increased, with 75 in 2013 (Ministry of Justice, 2015). The National Offender Management Service (NOMS) reviewed the ACCT process in 2010 and through various consultations with groups including safer custody teams, specialist staff, policy and operational managers, interested organizations, prison staff, healthcare staff, stakeholders and prisoners it showed that there was wide agreement about what parts were operating well and what parts needed strengthening. In particular, the areas for development involved revising and updating ACCT staff training, doing more to ensure requirements were fully understood, and that prisoners viewed the ACCT process in a more positive light and understood the process. Further, the proposals for radical change in screening, assessment, and care planning for those with mental health difficulties and those at an inflated risk of self-injury and suicide in English and Welsh prisons have been argued to have some face validity (Shaw and Turnbull, 2009).

Nevertheless, the extent to which these differing self-injury and suicide prevention measures over the last 20 years have been effective has been questioned and disentangling the specific causal factors can be difficult (Forrestor and Slade, 2013). Although the then suicide prevention and self-injury management *did* acknowledge the problem of SIDs in prison there appears to have been little impact as suicide rates continued to remain high (Wilson, 2005). The ACCT process seems to have been unduly focused upon identifying 'risk' when in practice only around one quarter of those who do complete suicide were deemed 'at-risk' (Liebling, 2007). But such criticisms need to be seen in the wider context especially given what we know about the fundamental limitations to a system based upon the predication of suicidal behaviour using data based upon a snapshot. Further, no comparisons appear to have been made with community care providers and the percentage of those who complete suicide who are actively being managed as at an inflated risk of suicide. There have been some downward movements with the rate of suicide over time but the rate of self-injury has remained at a high level in prisons (Ministry of Justice, 2010). In the female estate, the trend in self-injury has increased considerably (Ministry of Justice, 2010) and there is likely to be an underestimation of the actual figures given that rates of self-injury can be unreliable and staff reporting practices vary from prison to prison. The suicide rate in maximum-security prisons has increased, as has the self-injury rate in young offender institutions (Ministry of Justice, 2010).

The Harris Review (2015), which reported on SIDs of imprisoned 18 to 24-year-olds, concluded that there were serious shortcomings in not just the implementation of ACCTs (important though that is) but also the concept too. One key problem with the concept is that it is predicated upon the premise that those at an inflated risk of suicide are readily identifiable from those not. This sits uneasily with the observation that the various vulnerabilities associated with a higher suicidality are widely distributed across the prisoner population. Thus 'screening' tools will be prone to relatively high false positives and false negatives. A broader focus on the health and social care needs of the prisoner population makes far more sense to underpin effective policy and practice.

On a brighter note there are some early, and provisional, indications from recent research currently being concluded that the Prison Service may have been more effective in reducing the proportion of those taking their lives in the very early periods of custody. Research questions for the future would be, 'Have such deaths contributed to an overall reduction or delay in suicide?'. Either hypothesis, if demonstrated would be positive but of course one more so than the other.

Chapter Summary Points

- The Prison Service definition of suicide is more inclusive than those sometimes reported in community studies which, amongst other things, means a need for caution when making community comparisons.

- There remain definitional issues in much of the research into self-injury or 'self harm' which means again that we need some caution in interpreting such studies.

- Although there are some serious shortcomings to the implementation of the ACCTs there are also indications of some sterling work on the part of some prison staff in addressing this challenging area of practice.

Future Directions

Clearly there is much that could be done without any further research, in this book, as pointed out in the opening chapter we are not primarily arguing the need for further research but rather an evidence informed application of the considerable amount of research that we already know about. In short, at this juncture we would advocate investment in evidence informed services rather than the need for the further funding of researchers. The field is replete with evidence. We anticipate a key rôle for multi-agency collaboration, in which the assessment and protection of individuals vulnerable to self-injury and suicide is a product of effective teamwork rather than reliance upon one profession or the other. Collaboration and the exercising of joint responsibility between organizations is an important potential preventive measure, for both self-injury and suicide. Despite clear gains in the care of prisoners and prevention of self-injury and suicide in prisons in England and Wales, much work remains to be done. It can be argued that this base needs a renewed approach that seeks to understand better the connection between risk factors that individuals have at the time of entry to prison i.e. individual characteristics, social needs and the prison environment. Linked to this is a wider inclusion of practitioners who can listen to prisoners who are experiencing distress and pain, activate concern, and support to deliver joined-up care (Towl, 2000; Forrestor and Slade, 2013; Walker, 2015).

Further Reading

1. Bartlett, A.,Walker, T., Harty, M.A. and Abel, K. (2014). Health and Social Care Services for Women Offenders: Current Provision and a Future Model of Care. *Journal of Forensic Psychiatry and Psychology*, 25(6), 625-635.

    This article discusses the current secure provision for women in both the Criminal Justice System and the Health Service that has evolved over the last decade, in line with emerging gender-specific policy. It highlights the notable gains that have been made in approaches to self-injury in prison and the reduction in the high levels of secure hospital care. The authors suggest a reinvigorated model of gender-sensitive provision, which draws upon the principles of resilience and autonomy.

2. House of Commons Justice Select Committee (2013) *Women Offenders: After the Corston Report*, Online. ⟳ www.publications.parliament.uk/pa/cm201314/cmselect/cmjust/92/92.pdf
   In 2012, the Justice Select Committee began an inquiry to review the progress made since the Corston Report by examining current policy and practice relating to imprisoned women and adolescent girls and those at-risk of offending. The committee has now published its findings in *Women Offenders: After the Corston Report*. This briefing gives a summary of the committee's headline recommendations.

3. Towl, G., Snow, L. and McHugh, M. (2000) *Suicide in Prisons*. Plymouth: British Psychological Society.
   This book provided a review of the research into suicide and self-injury in prisons in the 1990s and made links between the research, the prison context, and related practice-based issues. It covers key issues for those working in the Prison Service in England and Wales at that time.

4. Towl, G. and Walker, T (2015). Prisoner suicide. *The Psychologist*, 2-5.
   This article considers the issue of rôles for psychologists in preventing prisoner suicide, and includes the perspectives of both the Prisons and Probation Ombudsman and a prison governor.

CHAPTER 3

Self-injury and Suicide Among Imprisoned Women and Adolescent Girls

Introduction

In this chapter we begin with an examination of the extent of self-injury and suicide in prison by women and adolescent girls in prison. The major research into self-injury in prisons is described; including that which has linked the risk of self-injury to a range of individual and environmental variables, for example, demographic factors such as age, ethnicity and situational factors such as type of prison and legal status of prisoners. There is also a discussion of those who are at highest risk of suicide where there has been rather less research. This chapter ends with a discussion of the motivations associated with self-injury for imprisoned women and adolescent girls.

Prevalence Rates

The need to address self-injurious behaviour in imprisoned women and adolescent girls has increased in recent years due to the growing numbers of such cases. As outlined in *Chapter 1*, over the last two decades there has been a marked increase in the number of imprisoned women. This increased between 1995 and 2015, from 1,979 to 3,932 respectively (Ministry of Justice, 2015). Some authors have referred to this as the 'new punitiveness', which has played a rôle in an increased number of SIDs in prisons by virtue of such increases in overall prisoner numbers (Towl and Walker, 2015). And such changes are more than structural, they are cultural too. Thus not only are there more women and adolescent girls in prisons but they are more likely to be viewed largely in terms of their convictions than to be viewed in a more rounded way as citizens with a range of aspects and needs. This is all part of the 'new punitiveness' (Towl and Walker, 2015). Even with this significant increase, women and adolescent girls in prison still represent around five per cent of the total prisoner population because the population of imprisoned men and adolescent boys has increased markedly too (Ministry of Justice, 2015). Historically one challenge has been to ensure that services for women and adolescent girls are not simply modelled on those for the gender-based majority but rather take account of sometimes differing gender-based needs.

There are difficulties in gathering accurate statistics on self-injury in the general population, this is because those who self-injure often tend to do so covertly and many episodes go unreported for many reasons and individuals may mostly not need hospital treatment. In the United Kingdom, self-injury is one of the top five causes of acute medical admission and those who engage in self-injury have a one in six chance of repeat attendance at accident and emergency within the year (Department of Health, 2012). In the 12 months to August 2012 hospitals admitted 110,960 cases of self-injury, and drug poisoning was the most common reason for self-injury hospital admission in England, almost nine out of ten admissions were for self-poisoning (89% or 99,200 admissions) (HSCIC, 2012).

Concerns have been expressed about the variability of recording practices, identification and the classification of what constitutes self-injuring and in particular when self-injury is different from a suicide attempt (Powis, 2002). The motivations for engaging in self-injury can vary and involve a range of factors. Practitioner's who have little experience of working with those who self-injure can find this a deeply frustrating area. This, in turn, may have contributed to the development of a sometimes pejorative nomenclature in relation to those who self-injure, for example, routine references to questioning the motivations of the individual captured with references to the individual as being 'manipulative' or 'attention seeking'. Such terms have no helpful place in the care of those who self-injure although can be commonly used even by experienced practitioners.

Methods of self-harm can be divided into two broad groups: self-poisoning and self-injury (NICE, 2012). However, it has been argued that there may be a range of diverse motivations and intentions behind the method chosen by individuals (Sutton, 2007). A further study found that there was evidence that individuals often change methods of self-injury (Lilley *et al*, 2008). Studies indicate that 80% of those who present at Accident and Emergency Departments after self-poisoning have taken an overdose of prescribed or over-the counter medication (Horrocks *et al*, 2003). In the general population self-injury has been found to possibly be more common than self-poisoning (Hawton *et al*, 2002; Meltzer *et al*, 2001). Cutting is the commonest self-injury method (Hawton *et al*, 2002; Horrocks *et al*, 2003) whilst stabbing, burning, hanging, swallowing or inserting objects, shooting, drowning, and jumping from heights or in front of vehicles are less common (NICE, 2012).

As highlighted in *Chapter 2*, studies of self-injury in prisoner populations indicate that imprisoned women and adolescent girls are at greater risk for self-injury than women in the community or male prisoners (Borrill *et al*, 2003; Gray *et al*, 2003; Klonsky, Oltmanns, and Turkheimer, 2003). A review in 2013 found that cutting and scratching were the most frequent self-injurious methods in both sexes; in imprisoned women and adolescent girls, self-strangulation was common (31% of all episodes) followed by hanging and self-strangulation (Crighton and Towl, 2002; Howard League, 2003; Hawton *et al*, 2013). The review found that most incidents were of low lethality, particularly in women and adolescent girl prisoners (Hawton *et al*, 2013).

Until 1997, the focus for reporting self-injury incidents in the prisoner population was as 'attempted suicide' but the problem with this approach was that prisoner intent was frequently unknown (Ministry of Justice, 2013b). Some incidents were more likely to be fatal than others but the point at which a self-injury incident became an attempted suicide was unclear. This is a genuinely difficult area. From 1997, all self-injury incidents had to be reported and this led to an increase in reported incidents in the prisoner population. Further, in 2002 a self-injury monitoring form was introduced based on the F213 'Injuries to Inmate' form (Ministry of Justice, 2013b). As a result, reporting of self-injury incidents improved further throughout 2003. The Ministry of Justice has now omitted self-injury statistics before 2004 from publications because it is considered, not unreasonably, that they were considerably under-reported compared with current standards. These improvements in recording practices have been important and a significant achievement in view of the pressures of a significantly expanding prisoner population as already described. In the 12 months to March 2015 there were 27,315 reported incidents of self-injury in prison, which is up by 3,786 incidents (16%) from the same period in 2014 (Ministry of Justice 2015b).

A case-control comparison of prisoners who self-injured and those who did not was undertaken between January 2006 and December 2009 in all prisons in England and Wales (Hawton *et al*, 2013). They found that 139,195 self-injury incidents were recorded in 26,510 individual prisoners between 2004 and 2009; 5–6% of imprisoned men and adolescent boys and 20–24% of imprisoned women and adolescent girls self-injured every year. Repetition of self-injury was common, particularly in women and adolescent girls, in whom a sub-group of 102 prisoners accounted for 17,307 episodes. Although it is true that the rates of recorded self-injury are higher for women than men. In terms of absolute numbers men and adolescent boys may well enact most cases of self-injury in prisons.

The recorded cases of self-injury for imprisoned women and adolescent girls have decreased from 2010 to 2012 and this was in part significantly driven by a reduction in the number of repetitive self-injurers within custody. This is unlikely to be a random event and more likely characterised by some high quality care from Prison Service staff. In the 12 months to June 2010 there were 35,300 per 100,000 prisoners self-injuring compared to 26,600 females per 100,000 prisoners in the 12 months to June 2013. In other words the rate has decreased from around one in three women to one in four engaging in self-injury. Although this is still a very high overall rate it surely reflects well on staff to have contributed to this significant reduction.

Suicide

Suicide is often the single most common cause of death in prison settings worldwide, with mortality rates more than three times higher than found in the general population (Hawton *et al*, 2013; Slade and Edelmann, 2013; Pratt *et al*, 2006; Shaw *et al*, 2004). The causes of suicide are complex (O'Connor and Nock, 2014; Task Force on Suicide, 1994) and are rarely the result of a single cause or event, but rather depend on the cumulative and interactive effects of a range of situational and psychosocial factors (Walker, 2015). Since 1991, the Prison Service has adopted the term SID to refer to all completed suicides in custody. This all-embracing description covers all deaths arising from non-natural causes that appeared to be directly caused by the actions of the individual concerned.

Few studies have addressed the problem of suicide among imprisoned women and adolescent girls. This is due in part to the small numbers in prison custody, which is approximately five per cent of the total prisoner population (Ministry of Justice, 2015b), but also because it is difficult to measure the extent of the phenomenon. Men complete suicide at a higher rate than women, on the basis of average daily populations (ADP) and receptions into prison (Crighton, 2000). It has been argued that being a woman or adolescent girl in custody increases the risk of suicide (Paton and Jenkins, 2005). When drawing comparisons with community studies the evidence seems to suggest that imprisoned women and adolescent girls are more likely to be given SID verdicts other than suicide (for example, open and death by misadventure) (Dooley, 1990; Liebling, 1994). Evidence also suggests that women and adolescent girls in prison are likely to be even more strongly selected for risk factors in suicide than the male prisoner population, in particular because of high levels of prior psychiatric contacts, alcohol and drug abuse, physical and sexual abuse which women and adolescent girls report in prison (Crighton, 2000). One challenge for the research is that the absolute overall numbers are thankfully comparatively statistically small for women so it is difficult to say definitively that men are at greater risk than women or vice-versa. However, the balance of evidence is that on average imprisoned men are at a greater risk of suicide than women although this does not mean that this will always be the case.

However, a review in 2015, contributed to by one of the authors of this work, which examined the number of SIDs in prison custody in England and Wales from 1978 to 2014, provides further support for men having, on average, higher rates of completed suicide than women (Ministry of Justice, 2015). This is the largest and most comprehensive such study to date both internationally and historically in the UK. There were a total of 2,014 SIDs from 1978 to 2013, and the average number of SIDs among male prisoners per year between 1978 and 2013 was 53, compared to three women's and adolescent girls' SIDs (Ministry of Justice, 2015). There were some years without any recorded SIDs for women in prison.

In relation to young adults in custody a review of 18–24-year-olds in NOMS custody (21% of the prisoner population) examined nearly 40 years of data on SIDs between 1978 and 2014 (Harris Review, 2015). The review, the first of its kind, found a total of 2,039 SIDs between 1978 and March 2014 (with 2,014 from 1978-2013 and an additional 25 in the first three months of 2014). A further 87 young people (four children and 83 young adults aged from 18 to 24) who died between April 2007 and December 2013 were analysed in detail as April 2007 was when the ACCT, the new care planning system for prisoners identified as at an inflated risk of suicide or self-harm, was introduced. With regard to gender and young adults in custody the review found once again that the women and adolescent girls constituted statistically small numbers.

Much of the work to date in this area of making such gender based comparisons has suffered from this common problem of being based on a small sample size and although in-depth qualitative analysis was used the findings are limited to how far they can be generalised in other prisons. Although the evidence has tended to indicate that men have higher rates of suicide in prison when compared with imprisoned women the data is by no means absolutely conclusive either side of the argument as the most recent large scale evidence as part of the Harris Review (2015) has indicated.

Risk Factors for Self-injury

The risk factors associated with self-injurious behaviour in imprisoned women and adolescent girls have been investigated to establish which prisoners are most likely to engage in self-injury and under what conditions. Statistically there are strong links between self-injury and risk of suicide.

Demographic profile

Differences have been reported for the rates of self-injury amongst different ethnic groups. The evidence indicates that the rates of self-injury are greater among Caucasians, in comparison with non-Caucasians, in both community and custodial samples (Borrill *et al,*2003; Gratz, 2006; Maden *et al*, 2000; Marzano, Fazel, Rivlin, and Hawton, 2010; O'Brien, Mortimer, Singleton, and Meltzer, 2003).

Having minimal intimate and close social support available within a prison has been found to be a risk factor for self-injury (Castille *et al,* 2007). A review of case records undertaken of 67 self-injuring prisoners compared with a random sample of 68 prisoners who did not engage in self-injury, three-quarters of the incidents took place in isolation cells or restrictive units (Jones, 1986). The author suggested the absence and removal of social support resulted in the increase risk of engaging in self-injury. Further to this, long prison sentences, being separated from family or being transferred against their wishes affected the high incidents of self-injuring rates of prisoner's (Dear *et al*, 2001; Liebling and Krarup, 1993; Haines and Williams, 1997).

Self-injurious behaviour in imprisoned women and adolescent girls has been linked to having a criminal history (Hawton *et al*, 2013). The results of a descriptive study undertaken of 78 women in custody who engaged in self-injury with a comparison group of 77 women who did not indicated that among those women who exhibited self-injury they were more likely to have an extensive and violent criminal history, and to have been imprisoned as a juvenile than imprisoned women who did not engage in self-injury (Wichmann *et al*, 2002). Being bullied or intimidated by other prisoners (Dear *et al*, 2001; Liebling and Krarup, 1993) were other contributing risk factors for imprisoned women and adolescent girls self-injuring. Other associated risk factors for imprisoned women and adolescent girls are having low self-esteem (Liebling, 1992), a reduced capacity to manage stress (deCatanzaro, 1981) and being young (Lloyd, Kelley and Hope, 1999). Self-injury has also been found to be more common in young prisoners (Hawton *et al*, 2013). Individuals younger than 20 years typically accounted for 13% of the prisoner population, yet 23% of male inmates and 21% of female prisoners who self-injured every year were in this age group. Self-injury in a correctional population has been linked to single marital status (Smith and Kaminski, 2010). Having a history of previous self-injury, and to have done this repeatedly, both in prison and outside were further characteristics linked to self-injury in prisoners (Abel *et al*, 2015; Marzano *et al*, 2010). Self-injury incident ratios (number of incidents/number of individuals) have found that imprisoned women and adolescent girls who self-injured did so about eight times a year whereas, male prisoners who self-injured did so twice a year on average, with little variation in this pattern over their study period (Hawton *et al*, 2013).

The relationship between childhood trauma and adulthood violence has been connected with self-injury, particularly for imprisoned women (Abel *et al*, 2015; Browne, Miller, and Maguin, 1999). Individuals with histories of a dysfunctional childhood (Rieger, 1971) and physical, emotional and sexual abuse (Wilkins and Coid, 1991) have been significantly more likely to engage in self-injury (Roe-Sepowitz, 2007). Lifetime self-injury was found to be positively correlated with a history of being physically assaulted, sexually assaulted, and experiencing violence from family and friends (Abel *et al*, 2015; Borrill *et al*, 2003).

Clinical factors

Various mental health disorders have been linked to self-injury in the literature. Depression and anxiety disorders are common co-occurring psychiatric disorders (Skegg, 2005; Klonsky, Oltmanns and Turkheimer, 2003; Haw, Hawton, Houston and Townsend, 2001; Trepal and Wester, 2007) and both are components of negative affect. In the literature, self-injury is often cited as giving relief from the build up of negative feelings and emotions, evidence indicates that imprisoned women and adolescent girls who self-injure have higher rates of depression and anxiety (Klonsky, Oltmanns, and Turkheimer, 2003). The concept of borderline personality disorder (BPD), which is reported as being characterised by rapid mood shifts, impulsivity, hostility and chaotic social relationships, is generally associated with self-injury too. It is one of the only mental health diagnoses in the DSM-5 (American Psychiatric Association, 2013) that includes self-injury and suicide attempts as criterion for diagnosis. In other words there is a need for caution in view of the potential for circularity. To assert that BPD is associated with self-injury when it is one of the criterion for such a diagnosis does not add much to our understanding but it is nonetheless worth being aware of in view of the powerful influence of the psychiatric establishment, personified perhaps in DSM-5, which includes diagnostic categories with no firm scientific basis. Sometimes it says more about professional (self) interests when we routinely regard people's distress as merely the symptom of diagnosable 'illnesses'. Such diagnoses often lack scientific validity (for a critique of this area see e.g. Kinderman, 2014).

Unsurprisingly perhaps, it has been found that individuals with a history of self-injury were almost twice as likely to present with signs and symptoms of BPD than those without a history of self-injury (Klonsky, Oltmanns and Turkheimer, 2003). Individuals with symptoms common with the diagnosis of post-traumatic stress disorder (PTSD), for example, numbing and avoidance, have also reported high rates of self-injury (Prinstein *et al*, 2008; Weierich and Nock, 2008; Zlotnick, Mattia, and Zimmerman, 1999). It has been noted that PTSD has received little attention in previous research on self-injury, suicidal behaviour and mental disorders in prisons (Marzano *et al*, 2010); however, a study in 2010 reported that PTSD was the third most prevalent diagnosis in imprisoned women and adolescent girls who had engaged in near-lethal self-injury, being diagnosed in approximately half of the sample (Marzano *et al*, 2010).

Substance dependence, particularly alcohol abuse, appears to exacerbate self-injury in individuals. This outcome has been established in both community and prisoner populations (Haycock, 1989; Karp *et al*, 1991; Wilkins and Coid, 1991; Haw, Hawton, Houston, and Townsend, 2001; Young, Justice, and Erdberg, 2006; Borril, Burnett, Atkins, Miller, Briggs, Weaver, and Maden, 2003). Other mental disorder diagnoses associated with self-injury include antisocial behaviour (Suyemoto, 1998) and eating disorders (Paul, Schroeter, Dahme, and Nutzinger, 2002). However, it has been highlighted that caution should be maintained with the association between eating disorders and high rates of self-injury because of the relatively low prevalence of eating disorders in prisoners (Marzano *et al*, 2010). In sum, we need to be cautious about such evidence (albeit mindful of it) in view of the questionable underlying support for the logic or validity of such diagnostic categories (Kinderman, 2014) and their evident circularity in some cases with self-injury in particular.

Institutional variables

A number of institutional variables have been studied in relation to self-injury. A key factor is the legal status of those who self-injure, and specifically the sentenced-versus-un-sentenced distinction. Studies have indicated high rates of self-injury amongst un-sentenced prisoners (Wool and Dooley, 1987) and having a life sentence (Hawton *et al*, 2013). These findings have some parallels with the research on suicide (see discussion later in this chapter). However, such studies can suffer from a common methodological limitation in calculating rates based on average daily population (ADP) in other words a snapshot design which will effectively serve to overweight remand status as a marker of suicidality rather than what more methodologically sophisticated studies have demonstrated, i.e. that it is time spent in the individual prison which is one of the highest correlates with risk of suicide as attested to as one of the most robust research findings historically and internationally rather than legal status per se.

There is evidence that the length of time a prisoner has spent in prison may be a key mediator with statistical evidence that just over ten per cent of suicides occurred within one day of arrival at the prison, with 45 per cent of deaths occurring within one month (Crighton and Towl, 1997). This view is supported by earlier research in Scotland (Bogue and Power, 1995) and is consistent with findings that report the rates of self-injury were found to be particularly high during early periods of custody (Loucks, 1998). For adult prisoners, several researchers maintain that around one-third of all incidents of self-injury are reported within the first seven days of reception into prison (Shaw *et al*, 2004). In a detailed study of prison suicides in England and Wales it was concluded that the period from reception into the main area was a time of very high risk of self-injury and suicide (Crighton and Towl, 1997). Thus, it may be considered that, at least to some extent, this may be independent of the overall amount of time spent in custody.

Other variables related to self-injury in the prison environmental setting are in relation to stress. It has been reported that if prisoners feel harassed or threatened and perceive a lack of freedom, boredom, isolation, and having limited future options the incidents of self-injury increase (Liebling, 1992). Further, behaviours in prison such as sleeping problems and lack of participation in activities have been found to increase an inmate's risk of self-injurious behaviour (Liebling and Krarup, 1993).

Psychological Functions for Self-injury

Incidents of self-injury may appear alike, however, they may serve an array of distinct functions (Jeglic *et al*, 2005). Self-injury may be seen as the result of *intrapersonal* or *interpersonal* reinforcement that can be characterised as being either positively or negatively reinforcing (Nock and Prinstein, 2004). However, it must be noted that self-injuring behaviour may serve a number of different functions at any given time (Suyemoto, 1998). Thus a range of unmet needs may be met through an act of self-injury.

Intrapersonal functions

Across a variety of settings ranging from community samples, women diagnosed as having BPD and adolescents, self-injurious behaviour has been found to serve the primary function of feeling a sense of relief from *unwanted emotions* and gaining emotional control (Briere and Gil, 1998; Brown *et al*, 2002; Gardner and Gardner, 1975; Nock and Prinstein, 2010). For the limited research undertaken within criminal justice contexts the results reveal that prisoners highlight an emotional regulatory function of self-injury. For instance, in qualitative studies, women prisoners described using self-injury to attain positive emotional relief (Walker *et al*, 2015; Kenning *et al*, 2010; Mangnall and Yurkovich, 2010). Forensic learning-disabled service users also described relief from unwelcome emotions as the primary reason for self-injury (Duperouzel and Fish, 2010).

In non-offender samples the feeling of anger has been found to precipitate self-injury (Brown *et al*, 2002; Herpertz, Sass, and Favazza, 1997) as well as among un-sentenced women prisoners (Wilkins and Coid, 1991). Negative emotions have been found to often precipitate self-injury, in particular, anger or aggression have been found to be primary precipitants of self-injury in custodial settings; 72% of self-injuring women and adolescent girls in prison presented with anger within 24 hours prior to their self-injury incident (Snow, 2002). Further work has examined the antecedents of self-injury compared to suicide attempts and it was concluded that negative feelings such as anger might trigger self-injury, whereas life stressors preceded suicide attempts (Miller and Fritzon, 2007; Snow, 2002). Imprisoned women and adolescent girls have also stated that anger is an emotion they feel prior to engaging in self-injury (Walker *et al*, 2015; Chapman and Dixon-Gordon, 2007). However, a limitation with these studies is that they were based on retrospective self-report.

Shame is another emotion linked to self-injury. In a sample of 89 imprisoned women and adolescent girls who engaged in self-injury over half identified shame as being a precipitating element (Milligan and Andrews, 2005). It must be noted that alternative patterns of self-injury occur within offender and non-offender samples. In particular, in relation to offending populations, self-injury was associated with impulsivity but not unhappiness (Hillbrand *et al*, 1996), whereas in community samples, self-injury was connected with unhappiness, but not impulsivity (Apter, Kotler, and Sevy, 1991).

Studies suggest that self-injury may primarily serve to relieve emotional suffering, particularly anger, in both custodial and community contexts (Klonsky, 2007). However, it must noted that if the *same* function is at play in both of these environments, questions need to be raised as to what is therefore accounting for the high prevalence rate of self-injury in prisons, particularly among women and adolescent girls. Several researchers have attributed the increased rate of self-injury amongst prisoners to either be the stress of incarceration (Paulus and Dzindolet, 1993) or a way of coping with the environment to handle intolerable feelings in the face of hopelessness associated with imprisonment (Dockley, 2001).

So, many commentators maintain that self-injury acts as a means of emotional regulation, but it is less clear *why* self-injury is used rather than another technique or strategy to escape aversive feelings. One suggestion is that self-injury may be ego-syntonic and acceptable because of how negatively the individual may feel towards themselves (Klonsky, 2008). For example, an invalidating environment in childhood may contribute to the self-directed resentment and self-derogation in those individuals who self-injure (Linehan, 1993; Klonsky *et al*, 2003). Results from studies in this area are mixed. Findings from studies with women with 'BPD samples' provide strong support for the self-punishment rôle of self-injury (Brown *et al*, 2002). For women in custody self-punishment as a function of self-injury has also been reported. Out of a sample of 50 imprisoned women and adolescent girls, 15 suggested that self-injury was a way of self-punishing (Miller and Fritzon, 2007). It must be noted that there are inconsistencies regarding the importance of the self-punishment function of self-injury.

Specific adaptive styles have been linked with self-injury. Among community samples, self-injury has been associated with avoidance, characterised by methods to escape particular thoughts, feelings or a stressor rather than engage in problem-solving (Chapman, Gratz, and Brown, 2006; Hasking, Momeni, and Swannell, 2008). Limited research has been undertaken in this area with criminal populations. In a comparison of incarcerated prisoners who self-injure with comparisons of prisoners who do not self-injure and non-prisoner control groups to assess strategies used to cope with real problems it was found that those who engaged in self-injury demonstrated more problem avoidance behaviours and had less perceived control over problem-solving options (Haines and Williams, 1997). Additionally, it has been reported that prisoners who engage in 'avoidance coping' are at greater risk of using self-injury on themselves (Kirchner *et al*, 2008).

Interpersonal functions

In the past, self-injury within criminal justice settings has been pejoratively referred to as 'manipulative' by some. It has been argued that any self-injury functions to have an impact on the environment, attract attention, or achieve some other goal has been considered manipulative (Dear, Thomson, and Hills, 2000). Numerous studies support this view, (DeHart, Smith, and Kaminski, 2009; Franklin, 1988; Pattison and Kahan, 1983), however, these studies used non-traditional means for operationalising 'manipulative' motives, such as if participants noted any reason other than suicide (Franklin, 1988). Despite this methodological issue, there may well be some value to the concept that prisoners may use self-injury for more interpersonal, relational and communicative functions, compared with individuals in the community. However, this does not serve to legitimate the use of pejorative nomenclature such as the attribution that an individual is being deemed 'manipulative'.

In a study conducted with 81 imprisoned women and adolescent girls emotional relief and escape were the most common reasons for self-injury, however, 'manipulation' was recorded as the third most common reason for a recent incident of self-injury (Dear *et al*, 2000). Readers may wish to consider whether this reflects more on the women and adolescent girls themselves or the staff writing such records. More indirectly, in a sample of 50 forensic mental health women service users 26% of the sample were categorised as having made threats and 28% a desire to transfer to another facility or another related environmental change just prior to their incident of self-injury, suggesting some communicative intent (Miller and Fritzon, 2007).

Relationship problems and difficulties are other risk factors associated with self-injury. A randomised controlled study, contributed to by one of the authors of this work, which piloted and evaluated a psychodynamic intervention for imprisoned women who self-injure from 2012 to 2015, provides some support for this link (Abel *et al*, 2015). Across three prison sites in England 113 baseline assessments were undertaken with imprisoned women and when the participants were self-reporting self-injury episodes many stated that the incidents seemed to follow a precipitant occurring in the relationships they had with partners, family and friends.

Rows, difficulties in close intimate relationships and problems of communication, especially with their elderly parents, were notable (Walker *et al*, 2015). Several studies therefore seem to suggest that interpersonal conflicts may serve as what may be termed proximal risk factors for self-injury among non-offender samples (Brodsky, Groves, Oquendo, Mann, and Stanley, 2006; Welch and Linehan, 2002). Comparably, it has been found that among offenders in a high-secure forensic mental health institution, the most common antecedent of self-injury was interpersonal conflict (42% of incidences) (Mannion, 2009).

Chapter summary points

- Imprisoned women and adolescent girls complete suicide at broadly similar rates to men, if in most years at generally lower rates.

- Imprisoned women and adolescent girls have higher rates of self-injury than men and adolescent boys.

- Imprisoned women and adolescent girls have higher rates of previous sexual abuse in their histories.

Future Directions

As indicated in the first chapter of this book a significant part of the future in suicide research, policy and practice needs to reflect a more nuanced understanding of the different groups who go on to complete suicide or engage in self-injurious behaviour. For example, the data seems to indicate that risk of suicide declines with age amongst women but increases with age amongst men. Policy makers and practitioners need to think through the implications of not just old and familiar findings but new findings such as these from the research.

Further Reading

1. Walker, T. (2015). Suicide and Self-Injury in Prisoners. In *Forensic Psychology*, Crighton D. A. and Towl G. J. (Eds.) Chichester: Wiley-Blackwell Textbooks.
    This chapter focuses on the individual vulnerable groups of prisoners who are at highest risk for self-injury and suicide. It ends with a brief discussion of current interventions and treatments in custody and the prison staff responses to prisoners at-risk of harm to self. Attention is also given in the chapter to some of the difficult methodological issues in this area of work.

2. Hawton, K., Linsell, L., Adeniji, T, *et al.* (2013). Self-harm in prisons in England and Wales: An epidemiological study of prevalence, risk factors, clustering, and subsequent suicide. *The Lancet,* 🔄 thelancet.com Published online September 16, 2013 🔄 dx.doi.org/10.1016/S0140-6736(13)62571-4.
    This paper reports on a case-control study of all prisoners in English and Welsh prisons to ascertain the prevalence of self-harm in this population, associated risk factors, clustering effects, and risk of subsequent suicide after self-harm.

3. Marzano, L., Fazel, S., Rivlin, A., and Hawton, K. (2010). Psychiatric disorders in women prisoners who have engaged in near-lethal self-harm: Case-control study. *The British Journal of Psychiatry*, 197, 219–226. doi:10.1192/bjp.bp.109.075424.
    This paper reports on the risk factors and indicators of vulnerability for imprisoned women from all the closed female prison establishments in England and Wales.

4. Humber N, Webb R, Piper M, Appleby L, Shaw J. (2013) A national case-control study of risk factors for suicide among prisoners in England and Wales. *Social Psychiatry and Psychiatric Epidemiology*; 48: 1177–85.
    This paper reports on the risk factors for suicide among prisoners in English and Welsh prisons between 2005 and 2008. Risks for clinical, custodial, service-response and socio-demographic characteristics are analysed.

5. Kinderman, P. (2014) *A Prescription For Psychiatry*, Palgrave Macmillan, London. This book is about human distress and calls into question our overreliance upon unscientific psychiatric diagnoses. Kinderman argues for an alternative model not predicated upon psychiatric diagnostic categories. Much of the literature on self-injury, particularly perhaps with women and adolescent girls draws heavily upon such dubious categorisation systems. So readers need to be aware of some of the limitations of such work.

CHAPTER 4

Supporting Women and Adolescent Girls with Poly-victimisation Histories in Custody

Overview

The majority of women in prison have extensive victimisation histories, including childhood abuse, intimate partner violence and violence from non-intimates and carers. The rates of women and adolescent girls in prison with sexual victimisation histories far exceed those of women in the general community. Furthermore, imprisoned women often describe episodes of poly-victimisation (multiple trauma) throughout their lives, including chronic and severe abuse. Many are therefore victims as well as perpetrators. In this chapter we explore the research base on best practice in supporting women and adolescent girls with poly-victimisation histories in the criminal justice system. We discuss the key challenges in providing support in these settings. We conclude with suggestions for approaches to support poly-victimised women and adolescent girls in prison.

Introduction

In recent years there appears to have been an increase in scholarly attention on women, adolescent girls and crime, however, very few studies have been based on primary sources from women and adolescent girls themselves in order to better understand their experiences. Here we begin by focusing upon the trauma histories of women and adolescent girls in prison. Specifically, focusing on the rôle of victimisation and traumatisation in the life histories of women and adolescent girls in prison.

Trauma Histories: Poly-victimised Imprisoned Women and Adolescent Girls

Trauma can be defined as any form of interpersonal or domestic physical, sexual or emotional abuse or neglect which is sufficiently damaging to cause prolonged physical, psychological or social distress to the individual (Moloney *et al*, 2009). Such adverse actions regularly, but by no means exclusively, occur within the context of familial dysfunction in combination with severe socio-economic disadvantage. This lack of outside resources and support structures may act to weaken the growth and development of resilience in individuals. Furthermore, complex trauma is characterised by severe and enduring victimisation that may lead to overwhelming feelings of worthlessness, hopelessness and powerlessness.

Women and adolescent girls in prison are far more likely to have experienced sexual and domestic violence than the general female population: evidence indicates that between 50% and 80% of imprisoned women report having experienced domestic and/or sexual abuse (Ministry of Justice, 2010b; Corston, 2007; Rumgay, 2004; Hooper, 2003). It has been reported that nearly half of all women in prison have suffered domestic violence and one third have experienced sexual abuse (The Social Exclusion Task Force, 2009). Qualitative research conducted with women and adolescent girls in prison has discovered significantly higher prevalence rates, and a study in 2009 revealed that around 80% of participants disclosed that they had experienced sexual and/or domestic violence (Women in Prison, 2009). A high prevalence of past and current domestic and sexual violence also exists amongst women on community-based sentences (Corston, 2007; Barnish, 2004). Similarly, research from America has indicated that imprisoned women currently convicted of violent offences, 'had significantly higher childhood physical and sexual abuse scores, and more recent abuse perpetrated against them than those convicted of non-violent crimes' (Brewer-Smyth, 2004:8). Thus, evidence indicates that imprisoned women and adolescent girls have extensive histories of physical and sexual abuse, which demonstrate *multiple* episodes of lifetime victimisation. In order to understand these multiple experiences of victimisation of women and adolescent girls in prison we will cover the concept of *poly-victimisation* more fully.

Poly-victimisation

Poly-victimisation was a term used by Finkelhor *et al.* (2005) based on research undertaken in America that used a developmental victimisation survey with 2,030 children aged 2–17 years. The survey explained the multiple and connected nature of child victimisation and to separate it from traditional child victimisation studies that regularly concentrated upon only *one* category of victimisation, such as physical abuse. By overlooking *poly-victimisation* Finkelhor *et al.* argued that this gave a potentially partial account, which underestimated the full extent of victimisation experienced. Those authors argued that previous research had confirmed that multiple victimisation is common, yet the inter-relationships between the differing kind of victimisation had not been sufficiently fully investigated. They also challenged the notion that by focusing on single victimisation, and even in the case of repeat cases with the same perpetrator and victim, there is a danger of over-emphasising the characteristics of single victimisation event or type, at the expense of a richer understanding of the wider profile of victimisation patterns.

In 2005 interviews were conducted with 100 women in prison regarding their exposure to victimisation and mental health functioning (Green *et al*, 2005). Nearly 98% of these women voiced traumatic exposure, most frequently violence from partners (71%) or childhood abuse (62%). Similar findings from qualitative interviews with 60 women in custody were reported several years later (DeHart, 2008). This research found that many of these women had experienced multiple victimisations, or *poly-victimisation,* in their lifetime and many explicitly connected traumatic experiences (for example, childhood sexual abuse) with the onset of criminal behaviours (for example using illicit drugs). It has been argued that the continued nature of multiple traumas in combination with further adverse childhood events (for example, abandonment, exploitation) normalises the behaviours for women such as exchanging sex for housing or drugs during adolescence (DeHart, 2008). A study in America found that 90% of 102 American imprisoned women reported sexual and physical violence from their partners in the 12 months prior to imprisonment, and that many women again described *poly-victimisation* (multiple trauma) throughout their life, including chronic and severe abuse (Lynch, Fritch, and Health, 2012).

In the United Kingdom the prison system has some groups of women that are over-represented, including black British women and foreign national women. In 2010 foreign national prisoners made up 20% of the female prisoner population and they came from countries such as China, Ghana, Jamaica, Nigeria, Pakistan, Romania and South Africa. From research undertaken with 103 such women 43 were identified as being victims of trafficking; five had entered the country independently, but had then been worked in slavery or servitude like conditions and ten had entered the United Kingdom in the hands of agents and been arrested following the theft of their relevant documents by their traffickers (Hales and Gelsthorpe, 2012). During the interviews with the women all of them described *poly-victimisation* (multiple trauma). It must be noted that the low levels of disclosure with women and adolescent girls in prison needs to be considered when reflecting on these figures, and it is probable that a higher number of imprisoned women and adolescent girls may well have experiences of previous multiple victimisation. A significant number of women come into custody with histories of pervasive poly-victimisation that far exceeds that of the general public (Mouzos and Makkai, 2004).

Effects of pervasive poly-victimisation on health and crime

With considerable poly-victimisation histories, it would be expected that there would be raised rates of post-traumatic stress disorder (PTSD) among women and adolescent girls in prison. Yet, evaluations of mental health problems with prisoner populations regularly omit PTSD prevalence (Fazel and Danesh, 2002). In response to this, a systematic literature review was undertaken with sentenced prisoners and it concluded that the frequency of PTSD in imprisoned women and adolescent girls surpassed that of the general population by a factor of six or ten in studies from New Zealand and Australia, respectively (Goff *et al*, 2007). In a study of nearly 1,500 imprisoned women and girls 30% stated they had been diagnosed with a mental disorder and that this was strongly connected to prior victimisation in childhood (Carlson and Shafer, 2010). Women and adolescent girls in prison with experiences of poly-victimisation are therefore at an increased risk of developing psychological problems, for example, depression, anxiety, suicide risk and PTSD (Turner, Finklehor and Ormrod, 2005).

Prisoner populations have an over-representation of individuals with substance misuse (SM) experiences. When investigating childhood victimisation and SM issues incarcerated individuals had 71% compared with 89% among male and female prisoners who had experienced victimisation as a child (Driessen *et al*, 2006). Childhood trauma precedes SM conditions and, it has been proposed, it may act as an adaptive strategy (Quina and Brown, 2007) or a form of self-medication (Brady, 2001; Khantzian, 1985) to hideaway from unresolved issues. The subsequent use of drugs and alcohol may then lead individuals to directly engage in drug-related offences or may increase their propensity for criminal behaviour. In Australia and America over half of the women imprisoned had used drugs and/or alcohol at the time of their offence (Johnson and Linking, 2004; Greenfeld and Snell, 2000).

Women and adolescent girls in prison who have issues with drug addiction and who have experienced previous childhood victimisation have a high risk of other adverse health issues (Messina and Grella, 2006): self-injury, suicide, psychological distress, use of mental health medication, eating disorders, alcoholism and prostitution. A study exploring the poly-victimisation histories of 480 offenders (188 females and 292 males) non-custodial offenders in Australia who were serving intensive correction or probation orders found support for such issues (Crime and Misconduct Commission, 2007). The study revealed that pervasive poly-victimisation was evident in childhood and was still continuing during adulthood at very high and varied rates among the sample. Mental health difficulties were prevalent in the sample; particularly depression and anxiety which were very high for women and adolescent girl respondents. Likewise, an association between self-injury and past victimisation has also been well documented (Abel *et al*, 2015; Gladstone *et al*, 2004; Van der Kolk, Perry, and Herman, 1991). In 2003 a study identified that more than one half (51%) of imprisoned women acknowledged engaging in self-injury in their lifetimes (Borrill *et al*, 2003). Further, the characteristics and predictors of self-injury among 256 women in prison participating in a 12-week trauma psychosocial intervention group were explored in 2007 (Roe-Sepowitz, 2007). In the self-injury group (*n*=109) women described more physical and sexual abuse, anxiety, and depression than those who did not self-injure. The author of that work argued that predictors of self-injury included a history of attempted suicide, sexual and emotional abuse and the diagnosis of eating disorders. Finally, another study found that for women in custody the number of childhood victimisation events was positively correlated with lifetime number of arrests, and negatively correlated with age of first arrest, first time in prostitution, and first property, drug-related and violent crime (Messina and Grella, 2006).

Whilst the interaction between poly-victimisation histories, law breaking and criminality appear established; the psychological mechanisms underlying these connections have remained largely speculative. The studies that document this cycle for women and adolescent girls draw accounts directly from the women themselves, mainly through them recounting their childhood and other life experiences and how this may be connected to their subsequent crimes. Some of the qualitative findings in this area will now be presented.

One of the early key papers identifying a connection between childhood victimisation and criminalisation was by Silbert and Pines (1981) who interviewed 200 current and former sex workers in America. Sixty per cent of the women in this study reported being sexually abused before the age of 16 mainly by men they knew. These women ran away from home, which led to prostitution, which almost always followed such early victimisation. The second study that explored this area interviewed 16 women in prison (Chesney-Lind and Rodriquez, 1983). It was found that half of the women had been raped as children and there was a prevalence of severe non-sexual child abuse experienced by ten of the sample. Links have also been made with women and adolescent girls in prison who have a history of childhood victimisation with later criminal activity (Arnold, 1990). Through using a mixed-methods study of 60 African American women in prison it was found that the majority had previously experienced violence. Another early study conducted illustrated a further link between victimisation and women's offending (Gilfus, 1992). Intensive interviews were undertaken with 20 imprisoned women and from analysing their life histories it were found the women moved from being a victim, to survivor, to offender. There may also be an increasing effect of poly-victimisation as a pathway to imprisonment for women and adolescent girls in prison (De Hart, 2008). Using qualitative analysis on the 60 interviews conducted with imprisoned women in a maximum security prison the author identified previous victimisation directly and indirectly that she curiously referred to as 'female criminogenic processes'. This observation was based on the borrowing of the pseudo-scientific term 'criminogenic' from the literature on men. (For a review of this term and its limitations see, e.g. Towl and Walker, 2015). But back to this research, it was found that child corruption, defensive or retaliatory reactions to trauma, and forced criminality were directly connected with some violent behaviour. The women described committing criminal acts in revenge for abuse and in response to threats of violence by intimate partners.

Taken together the above, chiefly qualitative, studies provide some interesting insights in informing our understanding of women and adolescent girls in prisons. In particular they lend further weight to the growing literature about the distinctive rôle of a history of poly-victimisation and trauma in women's imprisonment.

Effects of imprisonment on poly-victimised women and adolescent girls

Incarceration itself can have serious mental health consequences, especially for women with children and a history of poly-victimisation (Wolf, *et al*, 2007). Many women who have a history of poly-victimisation often experience a sense of powerlessness, worthlessness, hopelessness, low self-esteem and self-blame. Further, the links between previous victimisation and subsequent incidents of re-victimisation have also been well documented in research; these links represent a constellation of issues regarding women's mental health and wellbeing. Women and adolescent girls entering prison are therefore already vulnerable due to the prevalence and severity of their experiences of poly-victimisation and traumatisation. It has been argued that by being placed in prison they are in further vulnerable positions that damage their psychological and physical wellbeing (Girshick, 1999). Prison regimes may serve to intensify women's trauma while equally the trauma may worsen the prison experience for women (Baldwin, 2015; Moloney, Van den Bergh and Moller, 2009). Routine strip-searches for women and adolescent girls upon entry to prison and subsequently while serving their sentences have the potential to re-traumatise them. The everyday lack of privacy may well have a psychological impact too. Prison practices and operational procedures are frequently based on a male model, which routinely uphold an ethos of security, observation, containment, subordination and surveillance (Easteal, 2001). However, it must be noted that prison can also serve as a time of respite for some prisoners. The following section will now consider some of the possible effects of imprisonment on poly-victimised women and adolescent girls.

For women and adolescent girls in prison some of these policies and practices may trigger past experiences of abuse and violence and may be sources of re-traumatisation. Re-traumatisation happens when a situation, interaction, or environment that replicates or is analogous to the events or dynamics of the original trauma activates the overwhelming feelings and reactions associated with the initial trauma. During the original event the women will often have been powerless and therefore any situation in which they have no control over what happens to them can be re-traumatising. The standard polices and procedures that are used in prisons have been considered as having a re-traumatising effect for imprisoned women (Covington and Bloom, 2006).

It has been argued that a large number of the operating procedures of prisons are, unsurprisingly, not primarily designed to support the wellbeing and mental health of victims of violence and abuse; in fact they may be in direct conflict with such needs (Bloom *et al*, 2003). For example, while a key factor in the healing process for victims of sexual violence is to regain a sense of control in their life, in prisons there is a tension between the need for custodial control and the opportunities for the expression of personal autonomy, which may, on occasion have the impact of serving to reconstruct the structure of previous abusive relationships (Dirks, 2004). Exposing vulnerabilities, such as sexual abuse, within an environment that is hostile to healing may be at odds to prisoners' personal safety needs (Pollock and Brezina, 2006). For example, some women are perfectly understandably reticent about disclosing sexual abuse to authorities that they may not consider to be trustworthy, particularly because of negative encounters with such authorities in the past. Similarly, the use of group therapy approaches can be particularly problematic in a prison setting, as group therapy requires a safe and trusting environment. Other prisoners can use information within the prison system as currency, and information relating to traumatic experiences may be used against the traumatised young women in prison at a later point in time. As noted, 'in a prison environment, trusting other women with such information … is extremely problematic' (p. 98) as the 'prison sub-culture of non-disclosure and lack of trust' (p. 100) is in tension with the desired dynamics of group therapy (Pollock, 1998). Thus, disclosure of traumatic experiences such as sexual assault in a prison environment may directly impact on the safety and wellbeing of a prisoner during their period of incarceration and possibly have a re-traumatising effect.

There are a variety of other practices of prisons that may trigger re-traumatisation in prisoners. Firstly, as alluded to above, the use of what are now euphemistically referred to as full searches, previously known as strip-searches, on prisoners may be experienced as a form of sexual abuse insofar as they may cause them to 're-live' past experiences of physical and sexual trauma so they feel the same level of powerlessness and humiliation again that they felt at the time of the incident (Covington and Bloom, 2006). Further, the practice of full searching can be linked to PTSD and research studies indicate that the use of this custom does not fulfil its purpose as a security procedure and the detection of illegal imports or contraband remain low (Pereira, 2001; Fergus and Keel, 2005; Penfold, Turnbull, and Webster, 2005). Secondly, the use of restraint by prison officers or women and adolescent girls being segregated from the main wing so they are isolated (Blackburn, Mullings, and Arquart, 2008; Moloney *et al*, 2009). Thirdly, women and adolescent girls in prison being supervised by male staff when, for example, showering, dressing/undressing not only creates discomfort, but also can be extremely traumatic for women who have previous experiences of being abused by men (Moloney *et al*, 2009). Lastly, prison power dynamics are shaped by the structural division between those with formal power—prison staff—and those without power—imprisoned women and adolescent girls. As a consequence, this structural division of power is a constant reminder to women in custody that they have little ultimate independence or autonomy over their own wellbeing or bodies in this setting; thus reinforcing a sense of powerlessness. Of course similar points could be made about such women when service users in hospital if unwell but similarly dependent upon staff to access services.

Women and adolescent girls in prison often receive short-term custodial sentences and large proportions of them are on remand (Ministry of Justice, 2014). Due to the transitory nature of their stays, this can make it even more difficult to provide consistent and structured support in working with those who want to address their experiences of poly-victimisation. Firstly, due to many women entering prison with comparatively short sentences or on remand it may sometimes be impractical to undertake any meaningful therapy. Also for those on remand they may not be eligible to access some such services. Secondly, owing to the high prevalence of women moving in and out of prison there can be an increase in the feeling of hopelessness, insecurity and instability in relation to factors on the outside of prison, for example, with regard to childcare, housing and family matters. These feelings on entering into the prison environment may be heightened by the process of substance use withdrawal. Further, feelings of distress and uncertainty may also be heightened by episodes of self-injury, crises in mental health and suicide attempts. The movement in and out of the custodial system for women and adolescent girls may therefore be a time of great instability and some may experience this as a period of re-traumatisation.

Indeed we would argue that the major mental health issue for prisoners independently of gender is the adaptation to the life of the prison that they have been put in or transferred to. Adaptation to such changed circumstances requires a need to quickly familiarise oneself with new surroundings whilst having fewer social resources in terms of friendships and social relationships to draw upon to help meet such needs.

Supporting women and adolescent girls in prison with poly-victimisation histories

Examining and supporting imprisoned women and adolescent girls with their extensive poly-victimisation histories is an important topic for prison policy and practices. However, it has been suggested that it is impossible to engage in meaningful treatment with women and adolescent girls in prison on any issue, particularly abuse and trauma therapy, in a custodial setting because this environment cannot be therapeutic due to focusing on punishment and security (Baldry, 2009). This is an argument which is linked to a more general concern about the limitations of therapeutic work in prisons. Clearly there will be limitations to undertaking therapeutic work in the coercive setting of prisons. But we are not persuaded that it follows that there is thus no case for therapeutic work. There is, but with some limitations. It is important to note that prison can provide some stability, structure and respite for women and adolescent girls and may present an opportunity to engage them in support and interventions. Arguably this can be especially important for those who, prior to their imprisonment, had comparatively little structure to their lives.

Both positive and negative ways in which prison has impacted on women in prison's health have been identified (Plugge *et al*, 2006). Over a six-month period, 505 women were recruited from two remand prisons in England in 2004-05. Women were interviewed within 72 hours of being received into prison and then again at one month and three months. They answered questionnaires that explored 'subjective' health status, health related behaviours and health service use. Plugge and colleagues found that following reception into prison, some women's health and general functioning ('subjectively measured') improved. For example, the amount women smoked decreased, alcohol consumption and drug use decreased and fewer women exchanged sex for goods or money. However, there were no changes in exercise and diet and no statistically significant change in rates of self-injury for imprisoned women. The authors conclude that although the findings should be generalised with caution they do highlight the very poor health status of imprisoned women and indicate how, for some women, aspects of their health improve whilst in a prison setting. Nevertheless, it must be remembered that providing safety is the most essential aspect for victimisation and trauma recovery work and the prison setting cannot provide safety and stability in the longer term and sometimes not in the shorter term either.

There continues to be a notable dearth in health and prison policy directed to aiding women's recovery from poly-victimisation in custodial settings (Morris and Wilkinson, 1995; Chesney-Lind, 1998; McQuaid and Ehrenreich, 1998). It has been suggested that the change needed to attend to the pervasive experiences of poly-victimisation in the lives of women in prison needs to draw upon a feminist framework (Remer, 2003). Empowerment strategies should be within the prison so that women and adolescent girls can challenge the conditions of their lives that serve to devalue and subordinate them. Feminist researchers have tended to examine women's experiences in the broader context and aid individuals to unite their own experiences and actions to promote, 'resistance and personal integrity rather than infantilisation, self-directedness rather than conformity, and self-esteem rather than self-doubt' (Marcus-Mendoza *et al*, 1998, p. 81). It has been maintained that these aims present unique paradoxes in the environment of a prison (Hannah-Moffat, 2000) and the problems with putting forward feminist principles 'in custodial settings' and these criticisms need to be considered when developing prison policy. However, the notions of a feminist approach to empowerment and encouraging recovery from trauma have been recognised as an appropriate method for supporting women and adolescent girls in prison with poly-victimisation histories (Kendall, 1993). We agree.

In 2012, a paper was published that examined approaches to address women's victimisation histories in custodial settings (Stathopoulos, 2012). Although this work was concerned with sexual abuse and it focused mainly on Australian prisons, two of the frameworks highlighted appear to be promising interventions to deal with the poly-victimisation histories of women and adolescent girls in prison. The first framework involves that prison institutions approach the care of women and adolescent girls in custody from a *trauma informed care and practice framework*. Being 'trauma informed' means having knowledge of the rôle that victimisation has played in the life of the survivor (Harris and Fallot, 2001) and using this understanding 'to design service systems that accommodate the vulnerabilities of trauma survivors and allow services to be delivered in a way that will facilitate consumer participation in treatment' (p. 4). This framework is very different to *trauma-specific services* that are specifically designed to treat symptoms related to sexual or physical abuse or other trauma. Trauma-informed services provide all aspects of provision though a 'trauma lens' (Guarino, *et al*, 2009), not just those directly addressing the impacts of trauma. The focus is to generate an organization that understands the woman's past history and current experience of abuse from a holistic perspective; they view her symptoms in the context of her life and her traumatic experiences (Harris and Fallot, 2001).

Professionals must recognise that victimisation is often more than just a single event. It may include different types of trauma, repeated traumas, and/or multiple events that threaten a woman's worldview (Harris and Fallot, 2001). When a woman or adolescent girl is in prison their memories and feelings about their experiences of poly-victimisation may resurface or trigger new ones and this has the potential to result in overwhelming feelings of guilt and shame. The principles of trauma informed care include:

- understanding trauma and its impacts;
- promoting safety;
- ensuring cultural competence;
- supporting control, choice and autonomy;
- sharing power and governance;
- integrating care;
- promoting the knowledge that healing happens in relationships; and
- the idea that recovery is possible. (Stathopoulos, 2012)

Trauma informed care and practice within the prison system presents as a promising framework, but there is clearly a need to be mindful of security-related issues. We agree that caution should be advised because it would be inappropriate to operationalise trauma as a risk factor related to recidivism or prison misbehaviour rather than as a factor that determines women's needs, such as support or therapeutic intervention (Hannah-Moffatt, 2010). And this potential shines light on the nonsense of the concept of 'criminogenic factors'. There are factors, which contribute to our health, but we would not refer to them as 'healthogenic' factors. The term 'criminogenic' adds nothing useful to our understanding.

The second approach highlighted is a framework based upon gender-responsive principles (Stathopoulos, 2012). This framework aims to provide an overall approach to managing women and adolescent girls in prison (Covington and Bloom, 2006). Gender-responsiveness creates an environment through site and staff selection and programme development, content, and material that responds to individual women's lives and addresses their specific needs (Bloom and Covington, 2000). These approaches are multi-dimensional and are based on theoretical perspectives that acknowledge women's differing pathways into crime. The framework aims to address social and cultural factors, for example, poverty, race and gender and the therapeutic interventions involving issues such as trauma, victimisation, violence, relationships, substance misuse and co-occurring disorders (Bloom and Covington, 2000). It stresses that respect and safety should be central to how women and adolescent girls in prisons are treated. The main values of a gender-responsive framework are:

- acknowledge and accommodate differences between men and women;
- assess women's risk levels, needs, and strengths and construct supervision case plans accordingly;
- acknowledge the different pathways through which women enter the community corrections system;
- recognise the likelihood that women offenders have a significant history of victimisation;
- build on women's strengths and values, including recognising that relationships are important to women; and
- acknowledge and accommodate the likelihood that women are primary caregivers to a child or other dependent (Covington and Bloom, 2004).

In the women's prison estate in the United Kingdom, 'woman-centred' approaches are being encouraged which reflect many of the principles of the gender-responsive framework (Corston, 2007). Over the last decade, in particular since 2007 (Corston, 2007), attempts have been put forward by NOMS to improve the support prison and probation staff offer to imprisoned women and adolescent girls: Three policy documents are relevant here and they are listed below.

- Prison Service Order 4800 on Women Offenders (2008), giving guidance to prison staff on dealing with women who have experiences of domestic and sexual violence.

  ⟳ webarchive.nationalarchives.gov.uk/20110603043057/hmprisonservice. gov.uk/adviceandsupport/prison_life/femaleprisoners/

- The National Service Framework: Improving Services to Women Offenders (2010), a high level policy paper outlining principles and good practice and expectations.

  ⟳ webarchive.nationalarchives.gov.uk/20100303141250/http:/www. noms.homeoffice.gov.uk/news-publications-events/publications/strategy/ NSF-Women-08?view=Standard&pubID=558382

- Supporting Women Affected by Violence: Guidelines for Staff (2010) published by the Women and Young People's Team within NOMS.

  ⟳ www.womensaid.org.uk/core/core_picker/download.asp?id=3409

Nevertheless, despite the existing guidance, a review in 2011 indicated that there was still insufficient guidance on supporting women and adolescent girls in prison who had experienced domestic and sexual violence, despite the recommendations from the Corston report in 2007 (Women's Aid, 2011). The research base on the best practice for supporting women and adolescent girls with poly-victimisation histories in custodial settings is limited. It has been argued that prison governors are responding inconsistently, and activities in prisons are often dependent on the individual initiative of staff rather than a more structured and coherent strategic approach, which is evidence informed (Women's Aid, 2011; Bloom, Owen, and Covington, 2003). Inconsistency is not in and of itself problematic. Different approaches may serve to meet different needs. However there does need to be a consistency of standards in working with imprisoned women and adolescent girls.

Conclusion

As part of the new punitiveness in criminal justice more citizens are being imprisoned than in previous years (Towl and Walker, 2015). This includes women. The number of women in custody has been rising dramatically over the last 20 years and evidence indicates that many have poly-victimisation histories. Although these traumatic experiences may well not always be directly related to causing offending in women, they are considerably linked with women's pathways into criminality, such as substance misuse, sex working and mental health problems. Women's poly-victimisation histories are probably a key factor to be mindful of in developing future approaches to working with such women and adolescent girls.

Imprisoned women and adolescent girls have different needs than men and adolescent boys, and some policies and procedures found in prison environments may have a re-traumatising effect on women and adolescent girls in prison. Two possible ways forward have been presented. Firstly, the notion of trauma-informed care and practice that involves looking at all aspects of service provision with an understanding of the impact that poly-victimisation has on the lives of those affected. Secondly, the gender-responsive framework (Covington and Bloom, 2006) takes into account women's gendered pathways to offending and their gendered needs. Both of these frameworks require significant cultural shifts in the criminal justice system's policies and practices.

Chapter summary points

- If we are to better understand suicidality we need to better understand trauma.

- Imprisoned women and adolescent girls frequently suffer from multiple previous traumas. We need to think about the impacts of prison regimes on individuals who have been traumatised to move towards more trauma informed care. However, ideologically this may seem as at odds with the new punitiveness, which it needn't be.

Future directions

In recent years there has been some helpful guidance for working more effectively with imprisoned women and adolescent girls but this still needs building upon. But implementation and standards appear variable. Again, this is not an area that needs research as much as policy implementation and staff training so that staff can be more 'trauma aware' in their work with women and adolescent girls in prisons.

Further reading

1. Baldwin, L. (2015). *Mothering Justice: Working with Mothers in Criminal and Social Justice Settings*. Hook: Waterside Press.

   This edited book examines and discusses the reflections of experienced practitioners who work or have worked with mothers, both in and out of custodial settings. A spectrum of interventions are covered but in particular it urges the case for a whole new approach to women's imprisonment that draws upon trauma informed care and practice.

2. Covington, S. (2014) Creating gender-responsive and trauma informed services for women in the justice system *The Magistrate*, October/November 2014, Volume 70, Number 5, pp. 2-3. The Magistrates' Association: London, United Kingdom.

   This short paper gives details of research related to imprisoned women and their needs. It highlights that the criminal justice system has not adapted to meet women's needs, which often are quite different from those of men. The paper discusses the need for gender-responsive and trauma-informed services for women in prison.

3. Ministry of Justice (2009) *Short Study on Women Offenders.* Social Exclusion Task Force. London, Cabinet Office.

    This paper details a joint short study by the Cabinet Office and Ministry of Justice that examined how interventions, systems and services could be developed and improved to better meet the complex needs of women offenders.

4. Moloney, K., Van den Bergh, B. and Moller, L. (2009) Women in prison: The central issues of gender characteristics and trauma history. *Public Health* 123 426–430.

    This article discusses how it is critical that a better understanding is required so that services for women in prison can be achieved. The authors highlight that two key factors are needed if this is to happen. Firstly, prison policy needs to consider the demographics, determinants and profiles of imprisoned women. Secondly, an analysis of the rôle of trauma history needs to be part of these developments because it has a strong influence on offending behaviour. They conclude that any contemporary approach for women in prison needs to pay attention to these two important issues.

5. Wolf A, Silva F, Knight K, Javdani S. (2007) Responding to the health needs of female offenders. In: Rosemary Sheelan (Ed.). *What Works with Women Offenders.* Devon: Willan Publishing.

    This chapter discusses the health problems that imprisoned women encounter and the approaches that have been adopted to address these, often difficult, health needs. It focuses on the California Department of Corrections and Rehabilitation, which has moved forward in recent times in developing gender-responsive strategies. Health problems among imprisoned women are compared with both non-imprisoned women and imprisoned men and how imprisonment can further impact in various ways upon imprisoned women's wellbeing and health.

CHAPTER 5

Preventing Self-injury and Suicide

In this chapter we explore the recent trend in the United Kingdom to move away from a reliance on the identification of 'at-risk' prisoners to more proactive and positive strategies for women and adolescent girls in prison more generally who are suicidal and self-injure. This is followed by a discussion on contemporary approaches and interventions being used to support women prisoners who self-injure or are suicidal. This chapter finishes with examples of psychological interventions currently being used with women and adolescent girls in prison who have an inflated risk of suicide or who self-injure with a view to reducing their chances of completing suicide.

Moving Away from Using 'At-risk' Strategies

Approaches and strategies to prevent self-injury and suicide in prison have been suggested widely across the criminal justice process. It has been suggested that there are a variety of experts within the system who share the duty of care and responsibility for the wellbeing of those in custody, for example, police, prison officials, psychologists, psychiatrists and somewhat oddly criminologists (Biles, 1984). In the United Kingdom there has been a focused attempt to implement various strategies that move away from reliance on identification of at-risk prisoners to more proactive and positive approaches for those individuals in custody. This in some way is due to the difficulties of taking a 'medical model' approach to the prevention of self-injury and suicide in the prison context, which is based on the misplaced notion that those at-risk can be reliably identified at an initial screening stage and appropriate treatment offered. Even though suicide rates in prison are criticised as being too high, completed suicides in custody (and the community) have a statistically low baseline (Towl and Hudson, 1997). Consequently, while many individuals arriving at the prison may be identified as having the risk factors for both self-injury and suicide, only a small number will engage in these acts. So, screening and assessing the prisoner population would produce a large number of 'false positives'—that is, prisoners identified as having the factors connected with a higher risk but not actually going on to harm themselves. It may be argued that the issue with false positives can be managed by classifying fewer prisoners as potentially at-risk i.e. setting the criteria for inclusion in the group at a higher level. However, this would increase the likelihood of 'false negatives'—that is, prisoners who had not been screened as being a high risk but who subsequently go on to harm themselves.

The next part of this chapter provides current examples of preventative strategies directed at self-injury and suicide, which are in operation in English and Welsh prisons.

The Prison Environment

Prison policy has it that imprisoned men and women are treated broadly the same with regard to suicidality and self-injury. However, all prison governors and other staff in women's prisons are additionally required to comply with Prison Service Order 4800 (PSo 4800, 2008), which sets out gender specific standards for working with women and adolescent girls in prison. If appropriately implemented, these enable staff to be more sensitive to the gender specific issues that may affect women and adolescent girls in prison and respond appropriately. Further, in response to incidents of self-injury and suicide, the Ministry of Justice has attempted to reduce the prison stressors by easing the transition into the prison environment when women first enter custody, as detailed below.

Reception and first night

As already briefly mentioned in earlier chapters the prison reception area is a critical time for prisoners in relation to having a heightened risk of self-injury and suicide (Shaw *et al*, 2004; Towl and Crighton, 1998) as prisoners move into the care and control of Prison Service staff who have responsibility for their safety and welfare. It is very important that the reception staff receive accurate and detailed information about each prisoner, from staff at the courts, other prisons, probation, and health services. It is not unusual for prisoners to arrive late in the day with no information about their health from staff. Sometimes imprisoned women and adolescent girls may not have had sufficient food and drink during long drives across the country, between different courts and prisons. They may be concerned that their families have not been informed of their move or that there may be difficulties in getting visits. The reception processes have some different purposes in different types of prison; PSO 4800 states that women should not be required to wait for long periods in reception and the target for this process with imprisoned women and adolescent girls is that it should be completed within 45 minutes, which is shorter than the generic guidance that states the process should be completed in 2-3 hours.

On arrival at reception the national prison policy says that all new prisoners should complete a prison questionnaire at reception with a member of prison healthcare staff. The reception screen was initially developed in 2003 and was designed to screen for physical and mental health problems (Grubin *et al*, 2003). This screening method was rolled out across the prison system despite it having significant limitations in parallel with the main ACCT process (2004). During the screening process imprisoned women's and adolescent girls' previous self-injury/ suicide attempts and current ideation are undertaken as well as past medical history and current medical needs. This tool supplements basic questions on psychiatric history, purportedly allowing the identification of high-risk issues, such as self-injury and suicide in the first 48 hours of imprisonment (Humber *et al*, 2011). If self-injury/suicide risk is identified at reception the ACCT document is to be opened so that procedural monitoring and management can be initiated on individual imprisoned women and adolescent girls.

Evaluations have taken place of the initiatives that have been developed to improve the management of those at-risk of self-injury and suicide in prison (Humber *et al*, 2011). Using a before and after design they examined reception screening, clinical presentations of prisoners, care planning and mental health provision for prisoners at-risk in five prisons including three adult male local prisons; one female establishment and one male young offender institution. The results indicated that at reception, there was no change in the proportion of prisoners with suicidal ideation who were placed on the ACCT document, however, in prison, ACCTs were more likely to be opened following factors indicative of risk rather than actual self-injury and were more likely to contain better quality entries implying better care of and engagement with vulnerable prisoners. While under the care of the ACCT system, a higher number of prisoners were receiving primary mental health care input prior to ACCT implementation and prisoners on ACCT were more likely to be depressed but to be receiving no mental health care. ACCT closure reviews were significantly less likely after a prisoner was placed on this system.

Ideally imprisoned women and adolescent girls should be moved rapidly from reception through to the first night centres or wings designed to house prisoners new to prison for the first few days after arrival. The Prison Advice and Care Trust (PACT), a national charity that supports people affected by imprisonment, provides valuable services to newly arrived prisoners. These centres normally have higher prisoner to officer ratios allowing close supervision and are key to the early detection and prevention of mental distress known to be particularly acute in the early stage of imprisonment. The supportive environment allows new prisoners to share anxieties and concerns but also to receive a range of new information that aims to allow them to adapt effectively to prison life.

The Revolving Doors agency (2002) surveyed 1,400 women who had drawn upon the services offered by the First Night in Custody project. Imprisoned women and adolescent girls mainly presented with mental health needs that needed specialist services and their emotional suffering was intensified by the separation and lack of information about, their children. It was found that these centres permitted staff to assess the imprisoned women's immediate needs before they moved into the main prison (Dockley, 2008). Imprisoned women and adolescent girls feeling informed about what would happen to them during their first day in prison significantly improved, 23% in 2004 to 57% in 2006 and the number of prisoners who reported feeling safe on their first night increased from 56% in 2004 to 85% in 2006 (Dockley, 2008). It must be noted however, that criticisms have been made over the limited amenities and inadequate first night procedures to cope with vulnerable women (HM Inspectorate of Prisons, 2007). It has been convincingly argued that formalised first night procedures should be a central part of the Prison Service safer custody agenda (Dockley, 2008).

Social intervention

Social and physical isolation and lack of accessible supportive resources may intensify the risk of self-injury and suicide for women and adolescent girls in prison (Konrad *et al*, 2007). Consequently, it has been suggested that an important component in self-injury and suicide prevention in prison settings is meaningful social interaction (Kerkhof and Blaauw, 2007). A variety of accommodation strategies are employed within English and Welsh prisons as part of the management of prisoners who self-injure and/or who are suicidal. Preferably women should be housed in a dormitory or shared-cell accommodation with other women as findings indicate that this type of setting has positive results in reducing distress and episodes of harming themselves.

Another type of social support mechanism that is used in prison establishments is through the use of specially trained prisoner 'listeners'. This system relies upon prisoners trained in peer support skills and has been identified as an important tool in monitoring distress. In English and Welsh prisons the Samaritans have provided training for prisoners to become a listener and support prisoners in crisis. They appear to have a positive impact on the wellbeing of self-injuring or suicidal prisoners, as they seem to trust other prisoners more than professionals (Hall and Gabor, 2004; Junker, Beeler and Bates, 2005). In other schemes, peer supporters encourage prisoners to engage in educational activities or civic events such as wing-based committees or other special interest groups as these may balance the harm to confidence and self-esteem that may occur from the effects of prison life. It must be noted, however, that social interventions may also very well carry risks. For example, placing a suicidal prisoner in a shared cell may allow increased access to lethal tools and an uncaring cellmate may not warn or alert prison staff personnel if a suicide attempt is made. It has been maintained that putting prisoners who are suicidal into a shared cell must be carefully considered and not be an alternative to careful monitoring and social support by custodial staff (Liebling, 2006). For example see the inquiry into the death of Zahid Mubarek (2006) that reports on a racist attack by his cellmate, Robert Stewart at Feltham Young Offender Institution in 2000.

Imprisoned women and adolescent girls are encouraged to continue contact with their families, as this has been considered very important in balancing some of the anxiety and stress associated with imprisonment (Robinson, 2013). Visits in prison from relatives may not only sometimes go some way to prevent further re-offending but also can be critical to support women's and adolescent girls' psychological wellbeing so that they do not engage in self-injury (Robinson, 2013). However, many visitors' centres face critical funding shortfalls. Prisoners' families tend to be financially, as well as socially excluded, so these factors can lessen the chance and rate with which women receive visitors. Further, it has been found that families can experience frustration in arranging visits and may feel humiliated and upset by the attitude of staff and conditions of the visit (Loucks, 2002).

In 2013 the government published the *Women's Custodial Estate Review,* alongside their response to the Justice Select Committee report *Women Offenders: After the Corston Report.* These publications aimed to set out the approach the government proposes to take to managing women and adolescent girls in prison, in particular attention is given to ensuring that the custodial estate enables closeness to home and supports the maintenance of family connections. Further, under the government's Transforming Rehabilitation programme (Ministry of Justice, 2013c), all women's prisons will become resettlement prisons. This is intended to guarantee that women serving short sentences and those who are within six months of release are held closer to home and receive 'Through the Gate' support and statutory supervision after release. These developments are key as women are still imprisoned in a relatively small number of large establishments, and so many cannot be held close to home, for example, there is no women's prison in Wales.

Mental health treatment

A significant part of prevention strategies for self-injury and suicide in prisons involves regular assessments and interventions with prisoners by members of prison mental health in-reach teams. Over the last two decades the rôle of healthcare in the prison system has changed. Previously, prisoners identified as being at an inflated risk of injuring themselves were often isolated in prison healthcare and it was possible that for those who repetitively self-injured that this may have worsened their situation (Howard League, 2001). The changes in this area were highlighted in *Chapter 2*.

Purposeful activity

'Purposeful activity' within prisons encompasses various activities including time spent at work, education, training, physical education, and other activities such as offending behaviour programmes (HM Chief Inspector of Prisons, 2014). But it also includes time spent in exercise, in association with other inmates, and in basic tasks such as showering and using the phone (HM Chief Inspector of Prisons, 2014). These are designed to provide prisoners with constructive use of their time while in prison. Until 2004 the Prison Service set a key performance indicator (KPI) of 24 hours a week to be spent on these types of activities. However, due to prisons consistently failing to meet this target there was abandonment from 2004/5 onwards and it was managerially down graded to a key performance target (KPT) (Joyce, 2012). Currently, the KPT is for ten hours a day during weekdays for time-out-of-cell (HM Chief Inspector of Prisons, 2014). Good activity provision is often particularly important for women and adolescent girls in prison as it can improve mental health and wellbeing, and help vulnerable women and adolescent girls to settle into prison and recognise their capacity to learn and change (Rickford, 2003).

Although the Prison Service has a target to ensure prisoners are engaged in such activity outside of their cells, evaluations have illustrated that this target is very difficult to reach at times due to security issues, staff shortages, the sometimes poor management of resources, but particularly also if prisons are overcrowded. Surveys conducted on 6,500 prisoners in public sector prisons found that only around 12% said that they were able to be out of their cells for ten or more hours a day (HM Chief Inspector of Prisons, 2014). In a further study of 17 prisons in 2007 it was found that only three of the 17 prisons, even in the best possible scenario for a prisoner in employment, could provide the mandated ten hours a day out of the cell and none of the 17 came near to the ten-hour day for unemployed prisoners — who were a significant proportion in some of them. With regard to women and adolescent girls it was found that those who had engaged in suicide attempts often harmed themselves more when they had received cellular confinement (Rickford, 2003). Spending time-out-of-cells is imperative as was found in a study that examined self-injury among women and adolescent girls in prison (Borrill *et al*, 2005). Evidence has also illustrated that when time out of their cell occurs better experiences are described across many important parts of custodial life, for example, improved relations with staff, better access to healthcare and telephones, and more involvement in prison-based activities. They were also more likely to believe that as they had done something in prison that it would make them less likely to reoffend in the future (HM Inspectorate of Prisons, 2008). We therefore believe that it highly likely that there is a crucial association between time out of cell and prisoners harming themselves.

Bullying and safety

Bullying research within prisons has included more subtle victimisation behaviours in addition to physical violence, including social exclusion, verbal abuse, and gossiping (Ireland, 2000). Anywhere between 5% and 53% of prisoners have been bullied whilst in prison, dependent on the definition and methodology used (Ireland, 2002). Prison bullying research has focused largely on men; for example, evidence has shown that of 21 studies undertaken into bullying behaviour among prisoners from 1986 to 2000, only seven included women and adolescent girls (Ireland, 2001).

Bullying and intimidation among women and adolescent girls in custody is not usual. However those women and adolescent girls who engage in such conduct often, it has been argued, use less direct forms than male prisoners (Leddy and O'Connell, 2002). Of course whereas we have argued that overall there are likely to be benefits to greater out of cell and association time, one counterveiling risk is in the area of additional opportunities for bullies to bully which has, as we have seen elsewhere in this book been associated with an antecedent of greater suicidality. Women and adolescent girls are less likely to report direct forms of bullying behaviour than men (Ireland, 1999). One of the most detailed studies of female bullying was undertaken at Cornton Vale in Scotland and it was found that a quarter of the prisoners had been bullied at some time (Loucks, 1998). Physical violence was found to be infrequent in the study and bullying most commonly took the form of 'taxing', extortion and ostracism. It has been argued that imprisoned women and adolescent girls engage in more covert methods of bullying than man and it can therefore be difficult for custodial staff to detect (Leddy and O'Connell, 2002). It has been suggested that there is a connection between being a victim of bullying and suicidal behaviour in prison (Loucks, 1998) and it has also been found that levels of hopelessness in victims of intimidation and bullying were analogous to those in many clinical studies of severe depression and suicide (Evans *et al*, 1992; Macleod *et al*, 1993; Biggam and Power (1999). Other studies have also proposed links between victimisation and self-injury in prison (Power and Spencer, 1987; Liebling, 1992).

Over the last decade there has been a surge of interest regarding bullying in prisoners and a number of initiatives have been put in place by the prison system. In 1999, the requirement that all prisons should have an anti-bullying strategy became mandatory (Home Office Prison Service, 1999), demonstrating a commitment to deal with bullying nationwide. This was further developed in 2004 with the national policy on violence reduction (PSO 2750) that encourages a 'whole prison' approach to engage all disciplines of staff, as well as prisoners, in challenging unacceptable behaviour and improving personal safety and from 2008 there has been a policy of zero-tolerance to violence put forward by NOMS.

It must be noted that the Prison Service policy is not prescriptive in how violence is reduced in prisons rather it is at a strategic level, and it promotes an overarching approach to reducing violence in custody that is receptive to local needs. Strategies, although not prescriptive in their detail, the NOMS documentation proposes that they should include several key elements. Firstly, they must minimise violence through a number of techniques such as conflict resolution and problem-solving. Secondly, prisoners must be consulted about their views on reducing violence yearly. Thirdly, information and intelligence about all fights and assaults should be collated to identify problem areas and developing responsive action plans to improve safety. Lastly, prisons should also implement monitoring and evaluation procedures to measure progress. In recent years, the Prison Service has done much to address violence, bullying and safety, however, reviews and investigations still note that data was not always effectively used to identify patterns and themes, there was often no training provided about local procedures in this area and more effective reporting and recording of bullying among prisoners must be implemented within custody (Prison and Probation Ombudsman, 2011).

Psychological Interventions for Women and Adolescent Girls Who Self-injure in Prison

The most recent review of therapeutic interventions for women and adolescent girls who self-injure in prison was conducted in 2009 by NOMS (Ministry of Justice, 2009), and it reported that there were four programmes running across five establishments in the female prison estate. For example, there was The Carousel project at HMP Eastwood Park, a cognitive behavioural therapy based programme consisting of group and individual therapy sessions over an eight-week period and The Safe project, a problem-solving based therapy focusing on awareness and 'coping skills' run over three consecutive days, at HMP Bronzefield and Peterborough. These programmes are no longer running to the best of our knowledge. The main limitation to all of these self-injury interventions was that there was little evidence from evaluation studies. They had been instigated by psychological services within individual prisons rather than by specialist teams and the effectiveness of these programmes still remain unknown. However, notwithstanding their effectiveness or other-wise their existence did convey a willingness on the part of the governors of the prisons to prioritise engagement on meeting the needs of prison-ers as members of the public rather than the traditional narrow focus on simply reducing the risk of reoffending (important though this is).

Presently, NOMS does not provide any accredited psychological pro-grammes that are specifically designed to reduce self-injury in imprisoned women and adolescent girls (NOMS personal communication, 2015); however it does appear to be acknowledged that such programmes and other interventions could potentially contribute to improvements in women's and adolescent girls' sense of self-worth and self-efficacy, thereby reducing their risk of self-injury. Individual governors of some women and adolescent girls' prisons in England and Wales therefore continue to implement approaches that in some way address issues related to trauma. These innovative psychological interventions are covered below.

Options modified dialectical behaviour therapy

Options is a forensically modified-dialectical behaviour therapy (DBT) service set up by the clinical team at HMP YOI Holloway. This was specifically to treat women and adolescent girls diagnosed with border-line personality disorder (BPD) and/or antisocial personality disorder (ASPD) who are often excluded from treatment in prison and in the community. Putting aside the dubious logic of using such diagnoses as a basis for inclusion over need, the Options programme led on from the original Holloway Skills and Therapy (HoST) programme that was undertaken at the prison in 2008-2010, which was a three-year pilot funded by the Cabinet Office Social Exclusion Task Force and was pro-vided to women with BPD in prison. It attempted to address issues of offending behaviour, self-harm, suicidality and indiscipline through the use of DBT. This therapy is a cognitive-behavioural psychotherapeutic intervention developed in the late-1980s in America to help better treat those diagnosed with BPD (Linehan *et al*, 1999). It combines emotional regulation and reality testing techniques, with distress tolerance, accept-ance and mindfulness skills (Linehan *et al*, 1999).

HoSt adapted the original model of DBT because of the amount of movement by prisoners within and out of the prison estate. The pilot therefore used a shortened form of DBT which was modular, combined treatment of group and individual therapy and enabled women on short sentences or remand, or who were otherwise in prison only briefly, to benefit from learning some skills and receiving some degree of personal intervention (Gee and Reed, 2013). The results of the HoST programme found positive outcomes with regard to reduction in time spent on the ACCT process, reduction in adjudications; improved overall mental health and high percentage of client satisfaction (Gee and Reed, 2013). It must be noted, however, that of the 62 women accepted for the programme, only 29 clients finished one or more modules and further analysis across the two groups (clients who finished one or more modules and clients who dropped out before module completion) showed no difference between the populations (Gee and Reed, 2013). The HoST pilot was useful and provided some positive insights in this area; however, it used a small sample size and a small range of outcome measures.

The forensically modified-DBT Options programme was undertaken from November 2013 to June 2014 in HMP Holloway as a progression from the HoST programme, but with a specific focus on, targeting women and adolescent girls with BPD and/or ASPD. Women on the programme received an individual psychotherapy component, which spanned 18-19 weeks and focussed on problem-solving behaviours, priority was given to life-threatening behaviours, followed by behaviours that interfered with the therapy and finally, problem-solving quality of life issues. Women on the Options programme engaged in a pre-treatment phase of individual therapy two to three weeks before starting the group programme to orientate them to DBT, establish a commitment to the goals of treatment and the therapeutic alliance between the client and the therapist, as well as preparing the client for skills groups. Alongside the individual psychotherapy, women attended a skills-training group each week for 16 weeks. This aimed to enable women to control emotional regulation, manage interpersonal effectiveness, cope with stressful situations and develop mindfulness skills. There was a total of 26 women offenders who completed the Options programme and the findings indicated that women experienced a significant improvement in border-line symptomology and mood regulation, and a significant reduction in frequency of deliberate self-harm, days on ACCT and aggression to self and others after treatment. The treatment was also deemed highly acceptable to participants (Bartlett *et al*, 2014).

The findings from the Options programme have suggested some positive outcomes, however, it must be noted that there should be caution when interpreting these findings due to issues of insufficient evaluation rigour. The study only looked at one group of individuals, those who received the intervention. No control group was used and therefore no comparison can be made between those engaging in the intervention and a group who are not engaged in the intervention. It therefore lacks the rigour of a randomised control trial (RCT) a methodological omission common to sex offender treatment programmes in prisons in the United Kingdom too. Self-injury frequency was assessed via completion of ACCT forms which note the incident but fail to assess severity and this is an important factor when attempting to understand change in women who self-injure in custody. Lastly, the sample size was small in the study and it was confined to one prison, but this was a useful pilot study.

As with sex offender treatment in prisons in England and Wales, to-date, no study had used rigorous methods of evaluation to try and show a cause-effect relationship between treatment and outcome. To address this gap, in the summer of 2012 the Women Offenders Repeated Self Harm Intervention Pilot II (WORSHIP II) commenced, which one of the authors managed with Abel and colleagues, in three prisons holding women. This three year RCT investigated the efficacy of a brief psychological therapy, psychodynamic interpersonal therapy (PIT) (Guthrie *et al*, 2001), aimed at reducing repetitive self-injury and suicidal ideation in imprisoned women. This study and its findings will now be discussed.

Women Offenders Repeat Self-harm Intervention Pilot II (WORSHIP II)

WORSHIP II was an RCT study conducted in three female prisons in England and Wales (Abel *et al*, 2015). Women between the ages of 18 to 65 years were considered eligible if they were currently on an ACCT or had been on one recently, had a record of an act of self-injury in the last month, were in the prison establishment for a minimum of six weeks to complete the intervention sessions and were not receiving any other therapeutic intervention while in prison. Women meeting the inclusion criteria were invited via a letter to take part in the study by a clinical studies officers (CSOs). After a minimum of 24 hours the CSO would then discuss in detail the study. Discussions also took place with Safer Custody, custodial staff and in-reach mental health professionals about the participant's suitability, as electronic records were not always up-to-date regarding the women's progress in prison. After a woman gave signed consent, a range of baseline assessments were completed and, following these, the women were randomly assigned to treatment conditions. A minimisation method was used to ensure comparability of the two treatment conditions on age, prisoner status, previous reports of sexual abuse, previous contact with psychiatric services, alcohol problems, drug problems and self-harm before coming to prison. The Clinical Trials Unit, in London, undertook the randomisation process (Abel *et al*, 2015).

Women in the intervention group were offered 4-8 sessions of PIT. The therapy, developed by Hobson (1985), entailed identifying and helping to resolve interpersonal therapy difficulties, which cause or exacerbate psychological distress. In this study the PIT manual was modified for prison use but the empirical status of PIT is well established and there are high-quality efficacy and effectiveness studies of PIT (Shapiro *et al*, 1994; Shapiro, Rees and Barkham, 1995; Guthrie *et al*, 1999). In working with women who have repeatedly self-injured, the first task is to understand the circumstances that precipitated the episode. Importance is assigned to exploring feelings, and bringing these into the here and now. Problems, which are reported to have precipitated the 'self-harm' are studied and a shared narrative linking feelings, problems and relationships is developed. For this to occur a 'language of mutuality' is established; the therapist uses terms such as 'I' and 'we'. The therapist is active and the overall goal is to create a meaningful dialogue in which the therapist's suggestions can be worked with but adapted and owned by the client. Although the therapy work in WORSHIP II was brief, issues that arose between the therapist and the women were actively explored and linked to important relationships in her life. Sessions were offered weekly in the prison setting, lasted 50 minutes and were delivered by either a psychiatrist, mental health nurse, occupational therapist or a psychologist. All of these mental health practitioners had received PIT training. Treatment fidelity and adherence was ensured by weekly supervision, digital recording of interviews, and use of a standardised rating scale (Abel *et al*, 2015).

Women who were randomised to the 'treatment as usual' arm received an active control (AC) session that consisted of being taken out of their cells and having non-prison staff company. The AC participants had four sessions that occurred weekly, lasted 50 minutes and were delivered by the research assistant on the study or a CSO. Women were taken out of their cell and engaged in activities such as card games, reading magazines or practical topics (e.g. money management). No personal support was undertaken and women were aware that they could not talk about emotional topics. The author monitored and provided supervision for those involved in these sessions. Follow-up qualitative interviews were conducted at three or six months with a small sample of women who had completed: 12 PIT (six at three months and six at six months) and eight AC (six at three months and two at six months). The face-to-face interviews examined the feasibility of this process and assessed adherence, acceptability and ongoing skill usage post-intervention. Lastly, stakeholder interviews were undertaken with 14 female and male prison officers, safer custody and health care officers, mental health practitioners and governors. These qualitative interviews were to explore the acceptability of PIT in each of the prison settings. All of the interviews were thematically analysed. Methods to collect data on prison resource allocation incurred as a result of self-injury within the three prison sites was also explored.

A total of 113 women were randomised and assessed at baseline (PIT 56; AC 57) and 76 participants completed. For PIT there were 37 women (six completed two or fewer sessions and 31 completed three to four sessions) and for AC there were 39 women (nine completed two or fewer sessions, 30 completed three or more) (Abel *et al*, 2015). The overall aim of the study was to evaluate the PIT model that had been adapted for women's prisons to focus specifically on reducing thoughts and actions of self-harm, and suicide risk, in imprisoned women. Psychological assessments were completed from January 2013 to October 2014 on the 76 participants at baseline and post-therapy (Abel *et al*, 2015). The primary outcome measure was the total score on the Beck Scale for Suicidal Ideation (BSSI) (Beck *et al*, 1979) since strength of suicidal ideation is an important predictor of completed suicide. Depressive symptoms, levels of hopelessness, incidents, frequencies and severity of self-harming behaviours, screening for the presence of BPD and mental health history was also gained from the participants. Outcome assessments were analysed.

The pilot suggests that it was feasible to undertake a randomised controlled pilot for imprisoned women in three English prisons. Findings suggest that PIT and AC reduced thoughts of suicide, self-harm, self-harm repetition as well as self-harm severity post-therapy. The qualitative reports indicate that women in the PIT group continue to use skills learnt and PIT may reduce both number and severity of events during intervention (Abel *et al*, 2015). Very positive feedback, good practice and cross-agency working was reported from the stakeholder interviews. Outstanding work was also noted for the complex women completing PIT and how there were reductions in self-harm incidence, severity and ACCT openings for some participants of this experiment. Lastly, the stakeholders highlighted the benefits for AC women having weekly structured time too. Overall, WORSHIP II provided evidence of the feasibility and acceptability to deliver an RCT for PIT for repeat self-injury in imprisoned women, however, it has not illustrated that PIT intervention is better than active control: both reduced behavioural outcomes of self-harm repetition and severity. The intervention has shown promise at reducing behavioural outcomes of self-harm repetition and severity by self-report and PIT participants ongoing skill usage was evident.

Complicating Issues

Working with imprisoned women and adolescent girls who engage in self-injury and suicide may be complicated by the difficulty such behaviours presents for those providing treatment. The prison environment differs from healthcare settings in that the staff characteristically have less training in dealing with such challenges (Ivanoff and Hayes, 2001;

Short *et al*, 2009). Perhaps as a result of this lack of sufficient training and education, custodial staff may regard self-injury as manipulative (DeHart *et al*, 2009; Haycock, 1989; Kenning *et al*, 2010). A study that explored attitudes of prison staff towards imprisoned women who self-injure found that many staff resented women whom they believed engaged in self-injury for 'manipulation' and regarded these prisoners as less in need of support and care (Short *et al*, 2009). It is interesting how staff seem to want to distinguish between deserving and undeserving prisoners. This is not dissimilar to what sometimes happens in other health and social care services. With the views and beliefs that self-injury is used as an instrument for manipulation, this may add to the understanding that self-injury is unrelated to suicide risk (Snow, 1997). This interpretation stands in contrast to the finding that a history of self-injury is the most robust indicator of suicide (Joiner *et al*, 2005). Further, it has been found that prison staff also attribute self-injury to individual differences in women, rather than situational demands (Kenning *et al*, 2010).

Additionally, while many prison staff voiced compassionate views of those who self-injure the second most powerfully held opinion was that a punitive approach was an acceptable response to self-injury (Ireland and Quinn, 2007). The levels of stress in custodial environments may also inhibit the delivery of preventative treatment for self-injury and suicide. Staff in secure environments experience more stress than their peers in clinical settings and this stress is likely to be intensified by the higher rates of violence and aggression on staff by prisoners with a history of self-injury or suicidality (Young, Justice and Erdberg, 2006). However, we fully recognise that rates of violence are in general much lower in prisons than e.g. in accident and emergency units serving the general public. It was found when surveying support staff dealing with self-injury in prisons in England and Wales that the majority reported having support in the treatment of self-injury but that only half found the quality of support as representing best practice (Marzano and Adler, 2007). Lastly, despite the introduction of instructions, guidelines and handbooks (Gough, 2005; Pengelly *et al*, 2008) to support and direct staff so they can understand and manage self-injury in particular, it is unknown whether these are routinely used or indeed whether or not they are effective.

Chapter Summary Points

- There is a need for a move away from prediction and instead adopt a more public health based approach to prevention.

- All imprisoned women and adolescent girls have vulnerabilities especially in a prison environment.

- The focus on the first night and week in terms of giving support and encouraging positive social contacts needs to continue and be implemented with some consistency.

- Staff need to be worked with and supported in their work in this challenging area, with those who injure themselves or attempt suicide.

Future Directions

More staff support and training is needed as a bedrock of any suicide prevention programme. The management decision to not have suicide prevention as mandatory training for staff sent out a powerful and negative message about the value of the lives of prisoners. Our hope for the future is that that will be overturned. What could possibly be more important than saving lives in prison?

Further Reading

1. Abel, K., Shaw, J., Walker, T., Roberts, C. and Murphy, C. (2015) *Women Offenders Repeat Self-harm Intervention Pilot II* (WORSHIP II). National Institute for Health Research Research for Patient Benefit (RfPB) Programme Final Report Form.
This report provides the results of a three year study that piloted the use of psychodynamic interpersonal therapy (PIT) for imprisoned women who self-harmed in three female prisons in England. The results of the pilot carried out 2012/15 suggests a full randomised control trial of self-harm interventions with follow-up is feasible in imprisoned women and data suggests that the PIT can positively affect thoughts and behaviours of self-harm, potentially reducing suicide risk as well as reducing self-report self-harm attempts by imprisoned women.

2. Borrill. J., Snow, L., Medlicott, D., Teers, R. and Paton, J. (2005). Learning from 'near misses': Interviews with women who survived an incident of severe self-harm in prison. *Howard Journal*, 44 (1), 57-69.
This article describes qualitative research with women survivors of potentially lethal self-harm in prison. In-depth interviews were carried out during 2002/03 with 15 women (adults and young offenders) from six establishments. The interviews focused on the women's own accounts of the 'near miss' incident, including intentions and motivations, factors leading up to the incident, experiences of care and support, current self-harm and suicidality, and suggestions for prevention.

3. Konrad, N., Daigle, M.S., Daniel, A.E., Dear, G.E., Frottier, P., Hayes, L.M., Hayes LM, Kerkhof A, Liebling A. and Sarchiapone, M. (2007). Preventing suicide in prisons, Part 1: Recommendations from the international association for suicide prevention task force on suicide in prisons. *Crisis*, 28, 113–121.
In 2000 the Department of Mental Health of the World Health Organization (WHO) published a guide named Preventing Suicide. A Resource for Prison Officers as part of the WHO worldwide initiative for the prevention of suicide. In 2007 there are new epidemiological data on prison suicide, a more detailed discussion of risk factors accounting for the generally higher rate of suicide in correctional settings in comparison to the general population, and several strategies for developing screening instruments. As a first step, this paper presents an update of the WHO guide by the

Task Force on Suicide in Prisons, created by the International Association for Suicide Prevention.

4. Robinson, C. (2013) *Women's Custodial Estate Review*. National Offender Management Service.

This publication sets out the approach the government intends to take to managing women and adolescent girls in prison, with the aim of ensuring that the custodial estate facilitates closeness to home, improves resettlement opportunities, and supports the maintenance of family.

CHAPTER 6

Staff Training for Self-injury and Suicide

Overview

Since the Prison Service revised the suicide awareness strategy in the early-1990s training programmes have been developed. Although it should be noted that suicide prevention training is not classified as mandatory training in the Prison Service, it should be. This chapter reviews the staff training programmes devised for prison staff when managing prisoners who self-injure or have an inflated risk of suicide. Attention is also given to the impact on prison staff of working with prisoners in this area. The chapter concludes with some current research on resilience training and how this may be useful in the Prison Service.

Background

Between 2010 and 2013 the total number of prison officers working in English and Welsh prisons fell by almost a third, from 27,650 in August 2010 to 19,325 in September 2013 (Howard League, 2014). During these same periods the prisoner population was 85,200 (male prisoners 80,900 and women 4,300) in August 2010 and at the end of June 2013 there were a total of 83,842 prisoners (3,853 women and 79,989 male prisoners). Even allowing for overstaffing in places, some inappropriate interventions and inefficiencies in prisons, recent years have clearly been very challenging indeed. In some prisons, prison officer numbers have halved in the space of three years and some prisons have been closed or re-rôled as immigration removal centres, which has resulted in the loss of almost 6,500 prison places (Howard League, 2014). Over the same period figures from the Ministry of Justice have shown that the numbers of prisoners in each prison have either risen or been static (Howard League, 2014). This combination of fewer prison officers and less prison places has left much leaner prison officer staffing levels against a backdrop of a rising prisoner population. One caveat is that the changes in prisons have resulted in more contract management services. Thus there may be a greater proportion of staff who work with prisoners but are not directly employed by the Prison Service.

The Prison Service suffers from high staff sickness levels amongst prison officers. In 2011-12 the average number of working days lost due to staff sickness amongst prison officers was 9.8 days, this increased to 10.5 days in 2012-13 (Ministry of Justice, 2013). Staff turnover remains lower than the private prison sector for prison or custody officers. The average tenure of a Governing Governor in the public Prison Service is around three years four months (Hansard, 2013).

Prison Officer Training

Traditionally, prison officers were simply required to keep prisoners secure and ensure they behaved reasonably well. From the late 19th-century onwards, the purpose of imprisonment evolved from simple punishment to a process of moral reformation (House of Commons Justice Committee, 2009). The job of the prison officer has continued largely undefined (House of Commons Justice Committee, 2009) and it was only in 1935 that formal training for prison staff was introduced. The initial training primarily focused on the security aspects of the rôle rather than on rehabilitative elements. In 1991 Lord Woolf, the then Lord Chief Justice, undertook a significant review of the Prison Service following the riots in HMP Manchester. In his review it was highlighted that although there appeared to be a deep commitment from the majority of prison staff to the Prison Service, there were also levels of discontent and dissatisfaction. Prison staff expressed distrust and a lack confidence in the value of what they did (Prison Disturbances, 1990). Following the recommendations of the Woolf report a number of changes to the work both in terms of recruitment and selection and also the day-to-day rôle of the prison officer.

To join the public Prison Service in England and Wales individuals need to complete an application form, pass background and security checks and pass the Prison Officer Selection Test (POST), which checks an individual's number, reading and writing skills. There is also an assessment day, where individuals take part in rôle-plays to test how they deal with various situations, which are underpinned, by the testing of some core competencies to do the job (National Careers Service, 2015). If successful, individuals would start their training by completing the Prison Officer Entry Level Training (POELT) course, which is an *eight-week* course, aimed at giving the basic knowledge and skills needed to work as a prison officer. This training includes placements in a prison and a local training centre and also gaining knowledge and understanding on:

- professional standards
- teambuilding and interpersonal skills
- interviewing and report writing
- security and searching
- control and restraint techniques.

During the first year of service, prison officers continue to receive on-the-job training and are supported and assessed by experienced staff. They are also expected to complete the Level 3 (NVQ) Diploma in Custodial Care (National Careers Service, 2015). The United Kingdom's POELT prison officer training of eight weeks is possibly the shortest of all prison staff training in Europe and individuals do not require special academic entry qualifications or skills. It has been argued that the training emphasis more to do with security, fitness, strength, control and restraint, locking and unlocking and observing an adjudication process, and is not dissimilar in some ways to the rôle of a local community support police officer (Hanson, 2014). It has been argued that prison officers in recent years have been asked to undertake increasingly complex and varied tasks but have not benefited from commensurate remuneration, respect or support (Howard League for Penal Reform, 2009). The Howard League for Penal Reform (2009) proposed that being a prison officer should become a graduate rôle and that a requirement of A-levels should be imposed on new recruits. It is not however clear what the evidence is in support of these proposals.

In comparison, other countries train prison officers very differently and some argue that these countries offer more professional training. In Norway, prison officers complete a two-year training programme. To qualify for entry they must have entrance qualifications for higher education. Over the training period they must pass exams, and satisfactorily complete each placement and project work. After three years in post they must then complete a further week of training and most prisons also organize local training (Hanson, 2014). Similarly, in the Republic of Ireland prison officers have to successfully complete a two-year programme that leads to the award of a Higher Certificate in Custodial Care (HCCC) in order to become an established prison officer. The HCCC is a recognised third-level educational award at Level 6 on the Higher Education and Training Awards Council awards system. Overall, most prison administrations in European member states have some form of training for new recruits, although the length and quality of this training varies significantly. The length of initial training varies from a few weeks, as in English and Welsh prison system, to several years, as in Norway and Ireland. In some countries of Eastern Europe, such as Russia, the training of future senior prison staff involves the equivalent of a university course, lasting for up to four years.

Continued training and development

The continued training and development of prison staff is a critical component in the development of a modern Prison Service (Criminal Justice Inspection Northern Ireland, 2009). However, in 2003 the Prison Service put forward Prison Service Instruction (PSI) 09/2003 that abolished mandatory training, and a new training and development strategy was introduced. The strategy allowed the Governors to make decisions and decide on what training prison staff should receive locally and this would be based on the knowledge of the prison's business needs and resource constraints.

Following on from this, the Prison Service introduced PSI 22/2004 in April 2004 and this set out the arrangements for managing training locally and provided a framework to support the achievement of the audit baselines for training. The Training and Development Group (TDG) has a *Directory of Training* that provides details of courses that can be accessed by prison officers, however, most of these are 'ready-made' existing courses rather than 'bespoke' ones that have been written or adapted for need. Individual prisons also run courses for prison staff. Courses are kept under review and are frequently updated, altered or changed and all training courses in prison are continually examined and assessed to ensure the quality of content and delivery. The Course Review Panel examines and considers courses and when operational policies are introduced then the Operational Policy Group will identify whether it carries with it any consequential training needs. Lastly, the training delivered to prison officers is largely by the Prison Service's own trainers who have themselves been trained to deliver the training courses internally (Prison Service Instruction, 2004).

HM Prison Service training programmes for self-injury and suicide 1993 onwards

Suicide prevention training courses for prison officers have long been considered as crucial to decreasing the number of suicide attempts. Since 1993 there have been two official training packages developed for prison staff in England and Wales (HM Prison Service, 1993; 2001). The first was the strategy *Caring for the Suicidal in Custody* (HM Prison Service, 1993) that was established in collaboration with the Samaritans and launched in 1994 for prison staff in England and Wales. Training involved 14 hours of tuition across seven modules and the vital component of the policy was the move of the care of the suicidal prisoner from the medical model to a multi-disciplinary approach that used the F2052SH form (Hayes *et al*, 2008). This training received criticism on the grounds that there was far too much stress placed on the completion of paperwork (Hayes and Lever-Green, 2006).

Following on from this a thematic review was undertaken in 1999 by Her Majesty's Chief Inspector of Prisons (HMCIP) (1999) which highlighted that there was inadequate delivery and provision of training in local prisons, and it was further stated that 'there should be more of an emphasis on skills than an emphasis on risk factors, and rather than how to fill in forms' (HM Chief Inspector of Prisons, 1999). The Royal College of Psychiatrists responded to the 1999 thematic review, and their report in 2002 supported HMCIP's opinions. They argued that the recommendations from the review should be supported with regard to staff training and that this training should be aimed at increased suicide awareness among all the staff working in the prison estate.

In 2001, a revised suicide prevention strategy emerged from the Prison Service and this drew attention to the importance of equipping staff with the skills needed to work in this very complex and difficult area and all prison staff in all types of prisons should undertake basic, and if required refresher training as a matter of urgency (HM Prison Service, 2001). Paton (2007) found that the principal reason that prison staff were not attending training in this area was due to operational issues as Governors had difficulty prioritising this element of staff training. An attempt therefore followed that aimed to ensure that *all* staff received at least *some* training, and a 'core module' of suicide prevention was developed. This new training was two hours in length and it still included one hour and ten minutes on the use of the F2052SH paperwork form (Haynes and Lever-Green, 2006). This then left 50 minutes for staff to learn about why people may engage in self-injury, understand risk indicators, develop interviewing skills and explore some of the misconceptions and myths about suicide and self-injury. An examination of this new training was undertaken in more detail and it was argued that ultimately it continued to emphasise the culture of observation over interaction and remained reactive to self-injury and suicidal episodes or expressions of intent rather than being proactive (Haynes and Lever-Green, 2006). It would appear that this prison staff training continued to offer little for staff on how to approach prisoners who have a history of self-injury or suicidal prisoners.

Consequently, in 2003, the requirement for suicide prevention training was removed with the ending of centralised mandatory training for all prison staff (Prison Service Instruction, 2004). Training for prison staff for suicide prevention has been cited in other documents. For example, the first report by the Centre for Suicide Prevention at the University of Manchester (Shaw, Appleby and Baker, 2003) on deaths in custody, advocated that all members of prison staff should be trained in this area and risk management with an update on this course being provided to prison staff every three years. This team also highlighted that these types of training courses would need to be tailored so that they were flexible and adaptable to the demands of staff working in the prison environment, for example, with the introduction of modular courses tailored to working hours.

Overall, there was clear evidence in the literature at this time that there was a need for prison staff to be trained so they were sufficiently competent to assess the risk of self-injury and suicide among individuals at greatest risk in the prison setting.

Skills-based training on risk management (STORM) for prison staff

As discussed in earlier chapters, in 2001 the Prison Service extended its suicide prevention capacity creating the Safer Custody Group (SGC) and within this were new initiatives to improve the care and management of vulnerable prisoners. The Care of At-Risk Prisoners project, as it was known, highlighted that improved training in suicide prevention was an important aspect to this project, and in 2002, the SGC commissioned researchers at the University of Manchester to develop a version of an existing suicide prevention training package known as Skills-based Training On Risk Management (STORM) for prison staff. STORM was a training package in suicide prevention emphasising interviewing and assessment skills (Gask and Lever-Green, 2003). There have been two versions of STORM to date. The first version was developed as a generic package (Gask and Morriss, 1996) while Version II of STORM was established to accommodate and reflect practice changes (Lever-Green, 2007). The package is modular based with the opportunity to be flexible and adaptable to the needs of the organization. It utilises evidence-based teaching methods that are known to improve skills and confidence: rôle-rehearsal as well as videotaped rôle-rehearsal with structured feedback (Gask, 1998). Four modules cover the assessment of suicide risk, crisis management, and problem-solving and crisis prevention. Each module focuses on specific key skills to practice in rôle-rehearsal. *Table 1* (See the *Appendix* to this work) highlights in outline the STORM training package.

STORM has been evaluated since the late-1990s and to date there have been three evaluations in NHS settings. The first study involved two psychiatrists delivering training to 26 healthcare staff who had a range of different levels of education, experience and professional background (Morriss *et al*, 1999). Statistically significant improvements were found in participant's confidence, crisis prevention and risk assessment when dealing with people at-risk of suicide. A further evaluation of this training was undertaken in a much larger study whereupon two mental health nurses and one psychologist delivered training to 167 healthcare workers in a single health district over a six-months period (Appleby *et al*, 2000). This study found it was feasible to deliver training during a six-months training period and the results indicated that there were improvements in skills in the assessment and management of suicide risk and satisfaction with training was high.

Finally, the last evaluation undertaken of the STORM training involved it being delivered in three mental health services in England (Gask *et al*, 2006). Training was delivered by three mental health nurses during a six-months period in 2002 to 458 qualified and unqualified mental health care staff and data was collected over three time points: before and after the training and with a four-six months follow-up by post. The questionnaires assessed change in attitudes, confidence, acquisition of skills and satisfaction, the face-to-face interviews explored the impact on clinical practice and for the evaluation of skills training, participants were videotaped carrying out an assessment of a rôle-played service user. Findings showed positive changes in terms of attitude and confidence, but the study was unable to show improvements in skills or any demonstrable long-term benefits to skills in the participants.

These three evaluations have shown that STORM in NHS settings is feasible to deliver and can increase the confidence and attitudes when working and providing support to individuals in this complex area, however, it has not reduced the overall suicide rate (Morriss *et al*, 2005).

STORM continues to be implemented successfully across the United Kingdom and the Republic of Ireland.

Prison STORM was adapted from Version I and included a demonstration video comprising of prison specific vignettes and accompanying materials (Gask and Lever-Green, 2003) (⟳ www.stormskillstraining. co.uk). It was a standalone training package that sat alongside the ACCT documentation. The aim of Prison STORM was to help develop the skills needed to perform suicide assessment and management and it consisted of four modules, each of approximately two-and-a-half hours' duration (Hayes and Lever-Green, 2006). Prison STORM was conducted in three prison pilot sites between 2003 and 2004, and were evaluated at three male establishments, two holding adults aged 21 and over and one holding juvenile and young offenders aged up to 21 years old (Shaw *et al*, 2006; Hayes *et al*, 2008). A total of 182 prison staff accessed the prison training and they were asked to complete questionnaires immediately before and after training and at six-eight months follow-up. Each site delivered the training package suitable to their individual prisoner population requirements. At one prison site, the first two STORM modules were merged with locally developed 'empathy building sessions', while trainers at the juvenile and young offenders' site amended all the rôle-play case studies to be appropriate to their client group. Only one prison site used videotaped feedback as a standard part of the training.

The results illustrated that there were significant improvements demonstrated in staff attitudes toward suicide prevention, knowledge of risk issues, and confidence immediately following training. Satisfaction with the training was also extremely high. However, at follow-up there was a decline in knowledge and confidence, but the authors stated that this finding illustrated the importance of refresher training.

There are several limitations with the Prison STORM training that must be noted. Firstly, it did not include information on self-injury (Hayes *et al*, 2008). Secondly, it did not fit into the ACCT procedures efficiently as although the training presented how to assess risk and decide on action to address this, which was relevant to those who had an assessor rôle. However, the stand-alone nature of Prison STORM meant there was no information as to how the interviews shown in the videos related to the assessment and subsequent Care and Management Plan in the ACCT documentation (Hayes and Lever-Green, 2006). Lastly, there were differences in the implementation of the STORM training across the three pilot sites, for example, length of sessions and number of trainers/trainees in a session.

After the pilot training evaluation of Prison STORM between 2003 and 2004 and an interim evaluation of the Care of At-risk Prisoners project, conducted by the Safer Custody Group, training was acknowledged as being of key importance. Three packages were developed for various staff groups with minimum levels of training completion before the ACCT could be introduced to a new prison setting these were:

1. *ACCT Foundation Level*: devised by the Safer Custody Group that was compulsory for all members of staff. It was three hours' in duration and covered background information on suicide and self-injury in prison, and a description of the new ACCT processes and rôles and the format included a case study and rôle-play.

2. *ACCT Case Manager Level*: staff in this rôle completed one extra training day and this detailed sessions on care planning, case management and mental health awareness. The first two modules of STORM were retained as an optional module, so that the Governors of individual prisons could decide on its inclusion.

3. *ACCT Assessor Level*: staff in this rôle completed three days' of training, which included sessions on mental health awareness, care planning and ACCT rôles. In addition, it was mandatory for staff to complete either STORM or an alternative skills-based training programme (ASIST, Applied Suicide Intervention Skills Training). ASIST was a two-day course developed in Canada and approved by the World Health Organisation (WHO) and it required no previous mental health or suicide prevention experience. The training considered various myths of suicide, helped build relationships within teams, address the needs of different client groups and enable individuals to help persons at-risk of suicide. For staff

this brought the duration of the course to either four days (with STORM) or five days (with ASIST).

In 2006 the Prison Service decided to remove STORM as a compulsory element of the ACCT assessor training due to issues with funding the STORM trainers who delivered the training and an in-house package was then developed by the Safer Custody Group that focused more on the requirements of the ACCT policy as well as practical skills in the assessment and management of risk of suicide and self-injury (Hayes and Lever-Green, 2006).

Current framework for training in self-injury and suicide

Prison officers in the Prison Service currently receive a suite of training from the Safer Custody Group to ensure that they understand the NOMS strategy for managing suicide prevention, self-injury and violence management. The following courses are available to them (NOMS Learning and Development Group, 2015):

1. *Introduction to Safer Custody*: This course looks at the rôles and responsibilities with regard to the provision of safer custody, including legal requirements. The training ensures that prison officers understand the NOMS strategy for managing suicide prevention, self-injury and violence management. It looks at how staff can contribute to creating a safe and caring environment for offenders and topics examined include risks and triggers of suicide and self-injury, recognising distress, zero-tolerance to violence, raising concerns, record keeping, recognising stress and support available to staff. This training has been delivered since January 2012 and replaced the ACCT Foundation level.

2. *Introduction to Mental Health*: This training includes a general introduction to the area, covers misconceptions surrounding mental health and legal issues.

3. *ACCT Assessor Skills*: All officers receive training in the use of the ACCT system but the level of training they receive depends on their rôle and responsibilities within their prison. The ACCT Assessor training enables officers to deliver effective assessments of prisoners identified as being at-risk of suicide or self-injury.

4. *Safer Custody Case Manager*: This manager training enables officers to carry out comprehensive assessments of an individual's safety and wellbeing in a custodial setting.

5. *Enhanced Mental Health Awareness*: The course identifies signs and symptoms attributable to mental illness, how to maintain positive mental health, the basic types of care and management, referral practices and resources, care plans and where to find further information.

All new prison officers receive the training packages Introduction to Safer Custody and Introduction to Mental Health during their initial training. Local prisons then organize bespoke refresher training in Safer Custody, which focuses on any issues that each individual prison is currently encountering with suicide and self-injury. To date there has been no full-scale evaluation of the impact of this current framework for prison staff undertaken within the Prison Service, to the best of our knowledge. However, as illustrated above, studies have demonstrated that training can improve prison staffs' attitude and confidence when working with prisoners who engage in self-injury and suicide. Attention will now be given to the impact of dealing with self-injury, suicidal behaviour and suicide for prison staff.

Impact on Prison Staff Working with Self-injury and Suicide

Custodial staff in the Prison Service witness a high level of suicide and self-injury compared to staff in most work environments (Bennett, Crewe and Wahidin, 2008). The number of SIDs in prison increased to 87 self-inflicted in the 12 months to the end of September 2014 from 63 in the same period the previous year. Self-injury incidents across the prison estate increased to 27,315, which is up by 3,786 incidents (16%) from the same period in 2014 (Ministry of Justice, 2015b). The total number of deaths in prison custody increased to 235 in the 12 months to the end of September 2014 from 198 in the same period the previous year (Ministry of Justice, 2015). The impact of being employed within the prison setting has been argued to have shown that working as a prison officer may have an effect in terms of attitudes, feelings and behaviour (Arnold, 2005; Liebling, 1992). It has suggested that these effects can impact upon the domestic life of prison officers and can have a detrimental effect on staff wellbeing (Boudoukha *et al*, 2011). But it is not clear that such rôles have greater demands than a whole range of other health and social care rôles. There is sometimes a tendency for both prison staff and prison researchers to be somewhat insular in their perspective on such matters preferring to focus upon a perceived uniqueness of demands rather than their commonality with other health and social care workers.

Extensive ethnographic fieldwork was undertaken in 2004 in different types of prisons and interviews were conducted with prison officers, their husbands and wives and children to gain an understanding of the inner life of prisons in general and the working lives of prison officers (Crawley, 2004). This work illustrated what prison officers do but also how they feel about their work and in particular it highlighted how their experiences in prison impacted, often *negatively*, into their home lives and family relationships. The negative impact of working with complex individuals and how this may intrude on a professional's home life and their domestic relations has been supported further by other professionals employed within healthcare services and how they recount being affected by suicide (Alexander *et al*, 2000; Little, 1992). Equally, it must be noted, that there have been suggestions that not everyone who encounters trauma, observes traumatic events or works with complex individuals experience adverse after effects and, in fact, some professionals are able to use these experiences to produce *positive* outcomes such as post-traumatic growth and an enhanced sense of professional efficacy (Bonanno, 2004; Paton, Violanti and Smith, 2003).

Paton *et al* (2008) argues being a prison officer may be considered as a 'critical occupation' because observing 'critical incidents' such as self-injury and suicide can 'create a sense of psychological disequilibrium that represents that period when the existing interpretive frameworks or schemas that guide officers' expectations and actions have lost their capacity to organize experience in meaningful and manageable ways' (p 96). She maintains that the challenge is to pinpoint those features that can be developed before exposure to an adverse event or situation. Being able to predict an individual's capacity to develop a coping strategy will broaden their range of (unpredictable) experiences she maintains, so that when they do encounter them they can then address them in a meaningful and manageable way (Fredrickson, Tugade, Waugh and Larkin *et al*, 2003; Paton, 1994; 2006).

In 1983 the concept of 'emotional labour' was used to describe the things that workers do that goes beyond physical or mental duties (Hochschild, 1983). For example, showing a genuine concern for an individual's needs by smiling, and making positive eye-contact. Being able to create this 'publicly observable facial and bodily display' (Hochschild, 1983) is a necessary aspect of most public service rôles including within Prison Service (Newman, Guy and Mastracci, 2008). It has been argued that prison officers are conscious that they must play parts and effectively stage manage their emotions and actions if they are to regulate the impressions they communicate to prisoners and new officers to the prison setting have to learn the organization's 'emotional map' (Crawley, 2004).

Empirical studies have found that emotional labour had been found to have both positive and negative health effects on psychological wellbeing. On a positive level it has the capacity to allow workers to engage with clients or service users and gain job satisfaction (Grandey, 2000) whilst the negative effects have been linked with burnout (Kahn, 1993), emotional dissonance (Kruml, 1999), emotional exhaustion (Pugliesi, 1999) and alienation (Kruml and Geddes, 2000). It appears that a balance is therefore needed between engaging with clients, empathy and over-engagement to maintain the psychological wellbeing of prison staff (Slade and Lopresti, 2013).

Health care professionals' attitudes when working with suicidal service users have been shown to have an impact on the identification, management and prevention of suicidal behaviour, with positive attitudes leading to better outcomes (Neville and Roan 2013; Pompili, *et al*, 2005). Nevertheless, negative attitudes from professionals have the ability to disrupt these relationships and have a negative effect on suicide risk (Neville and Roan, 2013). Attitudes displayed by prison staff towards prisoners who engage in self-injury or suicidal behaviour has yet to be clearly defined, however, the limited prison studies that have investigated this area have found in relation to self-injury that staff often hold stereotypical attitudes and see it as a form of attention seeking and manipulation (Ireland and Quinn, 2007; Kenning *et al*, 2010; Liebling, 2002; Short *et al*, 2009). Furthermore, it has been argued that if prisoners are aware of these negative attitudes, they may cause further harm (Ciclitira, Adler, and Marzano, 2012). Such negative views of suicidal prisoners by staff probably make it less likely that prisoners will seek or receive help, thus reducing the opportunities to ensure that avoidable such deaths are not enacted. Prison staff therefore have an important rôle to play in the prevention of self-injury and suicide in imprisoned women and adolescent girls.

Chapter Summary Points

- There are some high quality training modules potentially available to prison staff, but they do not appear to be being implemented to all staff.

- It may be that governors would be more likely to meet such training targets if there was a specific individual financial incentive.

- Part of the training that we believe is needed is to support staff in their wellbeing in working in this challenging area.

Future Directions

We would repeat our previous exhortations that staff training is prioritised not just for the benefit of prisoners but staff themselves too. Staff need training in looking after their own wellbeing when working with traumatised imprisoned women and adolescent girls. They also need to have a research informed understanding of what we know about the factors associated with an increased risk of suicide and also protective factors which staff can potentially contribute to.

Further Reading

1. Crawley, E.M. (2004). *Doing Prison Work: The Public and Private Lives*. Cullompton: Willian Publishing.

    This book is based on extensive ethnographic fieldwork in different types of prisons and draws from interviews with prison officers' partners and children as well as prison officers themselves. It provides a sociological account of the world of the English prison officer, showing the job of the prison officer on a day-to-day basis and also explores their lives at home after work and their non-work relationships.

2. Liebling, A., Price, D. and Shefer, G. (2011) *The Prison Officer*, 2nd edition. Devon: Willan Publishing.

    This book is an updated version of the first edition of *The Prison Officer*. Through the use of a range of quantitative and qualitative data it explores the present rôle of the prison officer in Britain in an 'appreciative' way, taking into account the issues of power and discretion.

3. Howard League for Penal Reform. (2009) *Turnkeys or Professionals?* London: Howard League for Penal Reform.

    This paper discusses the complex and varied tasks that prison officers have to take in their jobs and suggests that a review is required of their rôle and highlights issues about the future rôle of prison staff.

4. Short, V., Cooper, J., Shaw, J., Kenning, C., Abel, K., & Chew-Graham, C. (2009). Custody vs care: Attitudes of prison staff to self-harm in women prisoners — a qualitative study. *Journal of Forensic Psychiatry and Psychology*, 20(3), 408-426. This paper presents qualitative research findings conducted with prison and healthcare staff in one English female prison. It highlights how women who self-harm are perceived by staff and their feelings towards working with women in prison day-in-day-out. Issues regarding training and support that is required for staff are also highlighted.

CHAPTER 7

The Aftermath of a Self-inflicted Death in Prison Custody

Overview

In this chapter we explore the impact of self-inflicted deaths (SIDs) in custody. The psychological impact of exposure to suicide in prisons is generally under-reported and there is comparatively little literature on it. Our focus is on the risk to prison staff, prisoners and the bereaved families too. We do not cover reputational or other such aspects of the aftermath of suicide; instead we focus on 'people-related issues'. However, the responsibilities of Prison Service staff in relation to SIDs in custody are briefly covered. We close the chapter with a consideration of possible future developments in this area.

Introduction

Since 2011 there has been an annual update of the recorded deaths in state custody by the Independent Advisory Panel (IAP) on Deaths in Custody, which gives independent advice to Ministers and prison staff leaders on measures to reduce the number and rate of deaths in custody (⊙ iapdeathsincustody.independent.gov.uk). The yearly report includes a breakdown of all recorded deaths in a wide range of custodial sectors including prisons and young offender institutions (YOIs). But, useful though such statistics and measures for potential systemic improvements are, we also need to consider the aftermath of such tragic events for those most closely involved. We know from data reported in earlier chapters that there were 2039 SIDs in prisons (including YOIs) recorded for the

36 years from January 1978 to March 2014 (Ministry of Justice, 2015). Of these deaths, there were more male SIDs in custody than of women and adolescent girls, with SIDs among male prisoners constituting 95% of all SIDs from 1978 to 2013 (Ministry of Justice, 2015).

It has been persuasively argued that some SIDs may well not be preventable; some individuals are determined to take their own lives and do so and some may be accidental (McHugh and Towl, 1997). When a suicide does occur whether potentially preventable or not it can have a significant impact upon the entire prison community. The average number of SIDs among male prisoners per year between 1978 and 2013 was 53, compared to three women and adolescent girls (Ministry of Justice, 2015). Overall, the large majority of SIDs in prison is broadly proportionate to the distribution of the genders, namely they are amongst males and the most common method used was hanging. In exploring such impacts we will first focus upon the wider context of bereavement whilst acknowledging that responses may vary greatly for specific individuals whether prisoner, staff or families.

Death, Bereavement and the Grief Process

Bereavement is defined as a state of loss resulting from death (National Bereavement Consortium, 2001) and grief has been conceptualised as 'the psychological and emotional reaction to bereavement' (Murray-Parkes, 2001: 23). Grief is a multi-faceted response to loss and it can include emotional, physical, cognitive, behavioural and social dimensions. While the terms are often used interchangeably, bereavement refers to the state of loss, and grief is the reaction to loss. Throughout life it has been argued that most individuals are exposed to at least one potentially life-threatening or violent event (Ozer, *et al*, 2003). Experiencing the death of others, e.g. a parent is part of the life cycle. Adapting to such potentially distressing situations can result in a range of responses some experiencing acute suffering from which they are unable to recover. Others experience such events less intensely and for shorter periods of time. Some individuals seem to recover quickly but then begin to experience health issues or difficulties concentrating or enjoying life.

Much of the study of the psychology of grief in the 20th-century has been ultimately credited to Freud (Walter, 1994). He developed in 1917 the concept of 'grief work', which was based on the premise that 'mourning has quite a precise task to perform; its function is to detach survivors' memories and hopes from the dead' (Freud, 1961: 253). However, Freud's theory was ill-defined (Stroebe and Stroebe, 1997). Bowlby (1961), built on the concept of grief work introduced by Freud, and developed a model that put into order the stages of grief. Briefly, it initially involved three phases: yearning and searching; disorganization and despair; and a degree of reorganization. In 1970 he worked collaboratively with Murray Parkes and a further phase was included—numbness. The fourth stage was based on research findings from a London study that involved clinical interviews with 22 widows aged from 26 to 65 years who were at various stages of bereavement (Bowlby and Murray Parkes, 1970). The model suggests that the first response is 'shock' and is characterised by feelings of 'numbness' that may last from a few hours to a week and it may be interrupted by outbursts of extreme anger or distress. Coping with every day tasks is difficult, due to incomprehension, denial and preoccupation with the loss. Following on from this is 'yearning and searching' for the lost figure, which can last months or, often years. This is a period of intense inner struggle in which awareness of the reality of death conflicts with a strong impulse to recover the lost person and the lost family structure. Next is 'disorganization and despair' whereby the individual has feelings of hopelessness and the grieving person is aware of the discrepancy between their inner model of the world and the world, which now exists. The last stage 'reorganization' involves the development of a new set of assumptions that includes finding a new personal identity; it is posited around a year after death. The last step in the recovery process is one of acceptance and the recognition that the person who has died will not be seen again. This model became known as the 'Grief Process' (Bowlby and Murray Parkes, 1970) and it had a major influence on healthcare professionals working with the bereaved (Davies, 2004).

The model of the Grief Process was adapted into a theory that described a five-stage response of terminally-ill patients' awareness of their impending death (Kubler-Ross, 1970):

- denial-dissociation-isolation
- anger
- bargaining
- depression
- acceptance.

The stage theory of grief put forward by Kubler-Ross became well-known and accepted, and has been generalised to a wide variety of losses, including clinical staffs' reactions to the death of an inpatient (Leiben-luft, Green and Giese, 1988). So, a sense of loss is fundamental to our understanding of bereavement. The loss of an imprisoned woman or adolescent girls can have potentially significant consequences for other prisoners, staff and the bereaved family.

Suicide bereavement

There has been a growing line of empirical inquiry that has centred upon both the examination of the effect of suicide on the subsequent grief experienced by suicide survivors (McIntosh and Kelly, 1992; Silverman, Range, and Overholser, 1994). The term 'suicide survivor' is used in the literature to denote those who have experienced the death by suicide of someone that they care about (Smolin and Guinan, 1993). Clinicians and researchers indicate that the bereavement process after suicide is different and more problematic than after other types of deaths (Clark and Goldney, 1995; Sprang and McNeil, 1995; Hauser, 1987) because those left behind often face unique challenges. In addition to the inevitable grief, sorrow, and disbelief typical of all grief, there may be an intensification of guilt, bewilderment, denial, embarrassment, and even fury may also be experienced (Jordan, 2008; 2001). These experiences may become more problematic by the effects of stigma (Feigelman, Gorman and Jordan, 2009) and trauma (Murphy, *et al*, 2003). Furthermore, the suicide bereaved are confronted with a death that is often unanticipated, untimely, often involves violent means and whether or not they are the one to find the body, may leave them with unpleasant images of the dead body (Shneidman, 1982). Thus bereavement is emotionally challenging for most of us but as we have seen such impacts may be amplified in the case of death by suicide. Coroners know this and some have argued that this has led to compassion informed decisions not to give a categorical verdict of suicide in some cases. Indeed this was one of the reasons why the Prison Service opted to have a more inclusive definition of suicide recorded as any SID. Thus to the credit of the organization there is very little chance of the publically-released figures showing an underestimate of the rates of prisoner suicides, unlike with some community-based studies which are sometimes reliant solely upon coroners' verdicts.

The characteristics of what is termed 'suicide bereavement' in the literature, have been outlined as being different from other forms of bereavement particularly, it is hypothesised because the suicide bereaved do not have time to prepare, psychologically or practically, for the death (Jordan, 2001). It is maintained that there may be the exhaustive search for *why* by suicide survivors, as suicide can seem such a meaningless act (Hauser, 1987). They may be questioning of their own responsibility to try and understand why they could have not done more to prevent such an outcome by replaying events, looking for clues and warnings that they blame themselves or others for not observing or taking seriously enough. The search for blame in these situations '… is likely to be enormously increased' (Bowlby, 1985: 6). An important issue is how individuals are considered as having control over their life and/or are persuaded or manipulated by others. For example, in custody, if a prisoner takes their life due to being a victim of bullying in prison, there will be concern and a need to seek blame is likely to be increased. This guilt can sometimes be manifested as blame where the survivor's own sense of accountability and feelings of guilt, it is argued, may be projected onto others and so others are deemed to be to blame for the death (Worden, 2003).

Feelings of guilt are a common emotional response in all kinds of bereavement, although it has been suggested that it may be more prevalent when the death was a suicide (Hauser, 1987). Guilt may also be displayed by using the phrase 'If only' to describe acts which might have helped to prevent the suicide (Worden, 2003). Added to that, guilt may also be felt because the suicide survivor may feel relieved (Clark and Goldney, 2000). A 'relief effect' for some survivors may be observed, for example, as they no longer have to cope with the deceased person's previous challenging behaviour, particularly perhaps if they had a history of suicide attempts (Worden, 2003). Guilty feelings may well be substantially less if the relationship between those remaining behind and the deceased had been good and problems could be discussed openly with one another (Kast, 1988).

Anger is a common response to loss and this may take many forms in its expression. In the case of suicide, it has been argued that anger may have three elements rejection, abandonment and accusation or as Lukas and Seidan (1987) states 'it is a rage at being rejected, at being abandoned and at being accused' (p.23). These feelings may be heightened if the death occurs in custody due to staff possibly feeling accused by their line managers of not having done a sufficiently good job, or indeed if they feel that they are responsible for the death. However, as with normal bereavement, survivors may be angry because the death was preventable, they feel abandoned by the deceased person, they are angry at a higher being, God, for allowing this to happen or towards friends and family for not being supportive enough. When the death is a suicide, anger towards the person may be more difficult as survivors may try to protect the positive memories they have of the individuals who died. Or as Toop puts it:

> 'Grief's anger has to show its face to be assuaged…guilt is present already and anger can unearth yet more guilt…a violent death compounds the difficulty. Parallel to anger there surges a deep need to idealise the dead….to erect the statue of a saint in place of a flawed human.' (Toop, 1996)

As discussed earlier, it is widely recognised (Bowlby and Parkes, 1970; Kubler-Ross, 1970) that in the 'normal bereavement' process the final phase involves acceptance and recovery. However, in suicide bereavements this may be more difficult, particularly in the custodial setting, with an arguably greater need for further information about the death.

Another area that is experienced by suicide survivors and not by other groups of bereaved people is shame and stigma (Silverman *et al*, 1994). Although not experienced by all survivors, these issues may be connected to cultural and religious contexts whereby it is believed that death by suicide brings humiliation, dishonour and disgrace on the whole family (Seguin, 1995).

In summary, it seems that there is evidence to support the view that the suicide bereavement process is different from other types of losses overall. That said, there are some significant individual differences in terms of grief response too, so what we are asserting is a generalisation but one we believe to be informed by the evidence.

Bereavement following a self-inflicted death in prison

The process for managing the aftermath of a suicide in the community and a suicide in prison can be different, however, the impact of such deaths on individuals is much the same. In most instances, any unanticipated death has a major effect on those involved, regardless of where it took place (Snow and McHugh, 2002). But, with a SID in prison, there are several extra dimensions that may cause stress upon those involved; these will be discussed shortly. It is important not to overlook prisoners and staff when an apparent suicide in prison custody occurs in the bereavement process because sadly sometimes the family support for prisoners may be absent and the prisoner's 'family' may in effect be the prison community. Mostly however, the family and friends of the prisoner will have a need to know the details of what led up to the untimely death of a loved one by suicide. As indicated above, any death in custody in England and Wales has to be investigated in public by a coroner and there are formal and bureaucratic processes. Inquests can be emotionally challenging for the families and friends, staff and other prisoners.

The Coroner Process, Inquest and Verdict

A coroner is an independent judicial official whose responsibility is to inquire into violent deaths, unnatural deaths, or deaths of unknown cause (Coroner's Society of England and Wales, 2012). The Coroners and Justice Act 2009 provided a number of structural changes to the coroner system in England and Wales and the provisions, rules and regulation made under this Act came into force in July 2013 (⊙ www.judiciary.gov. uk). The key points of which are illustrated below:

- Creation of a new national head of the coroner system, the office of Chief Coroner.
- Introduction of the new concept of 'investigations' into deaths, which where appropriate includes an inquest.
- New provisions relating to coroner areas, which correspond to local authority areas.
- Creating new titles for coroners.
- Removing barriers to where investigations can be held.
- New system of death certification (medical examiners).

Coroners must be legally qualified in England and Wales and they focus on the investigation of a death, which may include an inquest. Under the 2009 Act they do not have to open an inquest at a very early stage any more to allow for release of bodies and other such functions (⟳ www.judiciary.gov.uk).

If it is deemed by the coroner that an inquest is required then this must be completed within six months from the date on which the coroner is made aware of the death. The inquest that a coroner leads may involve a jury in order to identify the facts relating to the death before openly delivering a verdict, however this is not always necessary. All inquests must be held in public except where there is information that it may breach matters of national security (⟳ www.judiciary.gov.uk). A coroner's inquest is investigative in nature and the purpose is not to establish proof of liability, culpability or apportion blame, it is simply to establish the facts and circumstances of what happened in a fair and balanced manner. Although from a witness perspective it may well not always feel like a non-adversarial process as it is intended to be. Witnesses relevant to cases are called upon and they may be questioned to determine facts about the person who has died. The verdicts are very important in this process and in the case of a death in custody, there are a number of possible verdicts (Beckett, 1999):

- Killed unlawfully — the person was killed by an unlawful act by someone or some others as a result of their gross negligence.

- Misadventure — the person died as a result of actions by himself or herself or others that went wrong or had unintended consequences.
- Suicide — the person definitely intended to take his or her own life.
- Open verdict — there is insufficient evidence to return another verdict.

With regard to the verdict process, the Ministry of Justice (2011) has reported an increasing trend of coroners giving unclassified verdicts, for example, in 2010 these types of verdicts stood at 10% whilst nine years earlier in 2001 they were just 1%. An increasing number of coroners in England and Wales appear to be summarising their inquest conclusions with a 'narrative verdict', which records the circumstances of a death without attributing the cause to a named individual (Gunnell, Hawton and Kapur, 2011). An impact of the narrative verdict is that it can become an important tool in directing the attention of the court and the wider public to matters the coroner considers are of a public concern. Thus, such verdicts allow crucial concerns to be raised and can illuminate the shortcomings in processes or procedures of such agencies. With regard to the Prison Service for example, such supplementary comments may invariably impact on those who were formally responsible for the care, treatment and/or supervision of the person who completed suicide. Indeed a longstanding concern amongst some bereaved families and prison reform groups is that staff are rarely held to account in cases of suicide. When the same errors are repeatedly made with no apparent lessons learnt the Prison Service can come under criticism (Harris, 2015).

Having outlined the coroner process attention will now be given to exploring the impact of a death in custody from the differing perspectives of those who may be affected.

Self-inflicted Deaths in Prison and their Impact on Families, Prisoners and Staff

Various groups of individuals may be affected directly by a SID in prison custody. The experiences of the immediate family and friends of the prisoner who has taken his or her own life is understandably the most documented. The process of bereavement for family and friends may be hindered because their loved one has died in the prison environment with all the consequences of that as raised. At a vulnerable and difficult time they are faced with various restrictions in view of the bureaucracy required and law underpinning it. Immediate consequences can include it taking longer to gain even the most basic information, about their loved one. Delays can result from, e.g. the police examination of the scene to establish if a crime has been committed.

Bereaved families

The procedure of the coroner's inquest, outlined earlier, can be a source of distress for the family and friends of the person who has died (Hawton and Simkin, 2003) due, for example, to unanticipated changes in the information and accounts being given, which may be contradicted by witnesses and there is also the delay between the death and completion of the inquest. In the early-1980s there was a particularly large amount of dissatisfaction by bereaved families with procedures for dealing with deaths in custody and the failure of the State's response to these deaths. INQUEST was founded in 1981 and is the only charity in England and Wales that works directly with the families and friends of those who die in all forms of custody. It offers an independent free legal and advice service to bereaved people on inquest procedures and their rights in the coroner's court and the civil courts. And it appears that not only have they helped many bereaved families with legal and other social support but also that as a lobby group they have made some positive inroads to practice in terms of how bereaved families are treated.

In 2013 INQUEST conducted a detailed survey of bereaved family members who had used their service between 2010 and 2013. Using both quantitative and qualitative measures for gathering feedback and measuring impact the aim of the analysis was to see whether INQUEST had improved bereaved families' understanding of their rights, where to access quality advice and support and increased ability to participate in the inquest and investigation system. The survey also aimed to ask bereaved families about the impact of that assistance on their physical and mental health. A total of 3,336 family members completed the one-off survey and the results indicated that all families who were supported by INQUEST services during the time reported were helped to at least maintain their physical and/or mental health and 65% of those who used INQUEST services during the three year study reported a positive impact on their physical and mental health (INQUEST, 2013). This work concluded that the impact on bereaved families' mental health following a death in custody was clearly significant. For example, as would be expected, every participant in the sample described their enjoyment of life in the days after being informed about the death as poor and a significant number described their relationships with partners, family and friends as poor at that time (INQUEST, 2013). This evaluation therefore illustrated the positive impact of such work for bereaved families and how crucial it is that they are supported after a traumatic death in custody. There is therefore an ongoing need for further work in this area. We think that there is a case for that to be directly State funded possibly through the Department of Health.

Prisoners

Prisoners have both formal and informal relationships with staff and each other. When a SID occurs other prisoners can be, and frequently are, affected, particularly if they have been close friends with the prisoner, and a range of emotions, feelings and responses can be produced: disbelief, guilt, blame and self-scrutiny (Snow and McHugh, 2002). The bereavement process may very well and unsurprisingly therefore in fundamental respects be no different for prisoners than the impact of a suicide in the outside community. In order to support prisoners after a suicide in prison the Prison Service states it has peer support systems such as the Listeners, trained by the Samaritans, in place so that prisoners can talk in confidence to trained prisoners. This scheme was discussed in more detail in *Chapter 5*.

Limited research has investigated the impact of a SID in custody on prisoners. In 2014, the first qualitative study was undertaken to explore the experiences of young male prisoners who had witnessed other prisoners engaging in suicide-related behaviour (SRB) (Hales *et al,* 2014).

From the 70 interviews three main themes were identified: their experience of another's prisoners SRB; their beliefs of why the prisoner died by/attempted suicide; and the physical, emotional, and cognitive effects of another prisoners SRB on them. The support prisoners received from others after witnessing such events was explored, as were if they had any unmet needs, and their peers' responses were also described (Hales *et al,* 2014). An important finding was that over half of the sample described negative effects to witnessing another prisoners' SRB, which would suggest a need for support; however, many prisoners reported not having such a need. We would argue that more consideration of the support needs of prisoners is required who experience a SID in custody. This is hopefully an area for future development within prisons.

Prison staff

There has been some previous research investigating prison officers explanations of why prisoners engage in suicide and self-injury in prisons (Short *et al,* 2009; Lloyd, 1990; Liebling, 1992), however, exploring the *effect* and *impact* of a SID in custody on prison staff has only had limited research (Snow and McHugh, 2002). Prisoner and staff relationships are of critical importance, due to their interdependencies in the day-to-day routine work in the prison and through the personal officers scheme where officers become the first point of contact for information and advice. But much of the power of such relationships is predicated upon the asymmetrical power relationships between staff and prisoners. It has been argued that a suicide in prison custody may result in feelings parallel to those experienced following suicides in the community (Wright *et al,* 2006). In other words we would fully anticipate that the feelings of some prison staff would mirror the stages of bereavement that the prisoner's family goes through albeit, some have plausibly argued with probably less intensity (Lancaster, 2000; Snow and McHugh, 2002; Wright *et al,* 2006). In particular, the prison staff that are first on the scene may be profoundly affected, as unless rigor mortis has started to occur, they have to engage in immediate resuscitation in advance of the emergency services arriving (see Prison Service Instruction 64/2011 that details the management of prisoners at-risk of harm to self, to others and from others). It has been found that psychological distress amongst prison offices is at a higher level than reported in studies of professionals working on the frontline in the National Health Service, and, by default, the general population (Liebling *et al*, 2003). Of course this could be a product, to some degree, of the culture and how staff are recruited and trained. Also it may reflect a more resilient workforce in the NHS by comparison. The effect of prisoner suicide and/or self-injury was found to be one of the strongest contributors to that distress. Within the mental health and psychological literature it is widely acknowledge that by being exposed to suicide there is the potential for post-traumatic stress disorder (PTSD) to develop; an anxiety disorder caused by extremely stressful, frightening, traumatic or distressing events (Rogers *et al*, 2003).

Post Traumatic Stress Disorder

PTSD is known to impact upon an individual's ability to engage in effective social interaction in the workplace and withdrawal away from social support networks may occur as a result (Strauser and Lustig, 2001). Wright *et al.* (2006) state, 'an individuals environment may be conducive to that withdrawal' (p.166). Further support to this notion is highlighted by the fact that the custodial setting produces a 'predominantly machismo culture', which frequently, 'militates against the acknowledgement of adverse reactions, normal though they may be' (Snow and McHugh, 2002, p. 151). Prison officers are therefore meant to be strong individuals, able to 'handle' incidents that would be stressful for the general population, and not disclose their distress, as doing so may result in emotional isolation from their colleagues (Wright *et al*, 2006). One study involved exploring 38 deaths in the South Australian prison system from 1 January 1980 to 31 March 1993 and the impact they had on staff, other prisoners, families and friends of the prisoners concerned (Dawes, 1999). This study showed that as far back as the early-1980s it was seen as inappropriate for staff to grieve openly and display distress at the suicide of a prisoner. It was also found that staff were concerned about the reaction of colleagues if they did display emotions. It is important that supportive interventions are created within the Prison Service to both help distressed and possibly PTSD suffering staff, and improve the negative aspects of the prison officer culture. Paradoxically such a culture may contribute to reducing the resilience of staff, as we have seen when compared to reports around health service workers.

A study conducted in the United Kingdom with prison officers in 2006 explored the incidence of PTSD in 49 women and men prison staff who had experienced a prisoner suicide in custody in the period three-seven months prior to the study commencing (Wright *et al*, 2006). It used a cross-sectional survey design employing a self-report questionnaire, which was administered as part of a semi-structured interview. They found that 18 of the 49 participants scored over the cut-off point on the trauma factor of the Traumatic Symptom Inventory (Briere, 1995), which means participants were displaying clinical level symptoms of PTSD. The authors assert that the incidence rate of 37% is high and that this identifies a problem, which needs to be addressed. However, despite such assertions there is often much less clarity from researchers in the field as to how such issues may be addressed in concrete terms for improvements. Further, they indicate that this rate may be even higher as there was a number of prison officers who declined to participate because they had been diagnosed as being clinically affected by a SID in custody and were signed-off work by a health professional. The authors highlight that the sample is small but they do conclude that this is an area that requires further study due to a significant percentage of prison officers showing that they had been affected by a death in custody and were not receiving the care that they required (Wright *et al*, 2006). In conclusion it may be that preventive measures rather than targeted treatment interventions after the event should be used to help staff deal with SIDs in custody. Preventative measures for staff could include sessions on resilience and wellbeing early during the training cycle of prison staff as well as working towards reducing the numbers of SIDs in prisons.

In 2010, the Prison Service issued a new Prison Service Instruction (PSI) for Post Incident Care (08/2010) that had been informed by the then National Institute for Clinical Excellence (NICE) guidelines for the management of PTSD. This was an important step for NOMS as it recognised prison staff were at an increased risk of experiencing traumatic events in the workplace compared to many other occupations and this

PSI explicitly stated that one of the situations where this may occur is when there is a violent death of a prisoner, either self-inflicted or at the hands of a third party. The policy then identifies a series of procedures that should be followed for staff who have been directly involved in an incident that has a clear risk of traumatic exposure, these are highlighted below:

- Identified and shared information on post-trauma stress disorder (PTSD) that NOMS has produced.
- Given a 'hot' debrief before going off duty, which acknowledges what happened, the rôle of the staff involved, attempts to normalise the situation and ensure that immediate needs of the staff have been met.
- Referred to, and supported by, the establishment's care team who provides one-to-one, confidential and discreet peer support to staff who have been involved in the incident.
- Where appropriate, assessed for risk of developing long-term post-trauma stress symptoms.
- Offered appropriate support and specialist interventions if required.

According to Prison Service policies within five-ten days of a potentially traumatic incident a Critical Incident Debrief will also take place and will give staff the opportunity to discuss the personal impact of the incident with others involved, provide information on the effects and normalisation of post-trauma stress and its reactions. The debrief will also encourage coping strategies and support networks. The process of PSI (08/2010) for post incident care presents as clear and supportive, however caution is needed as being referred to and supported by the prison care team may be very difficult for prison staff as disclosing work-related stress, it has been argued, is highly stigmatised in the Prison Service (Kinman, Clements and Hart, 2015). Furthermore, there is some evidence that indicates many prison staff feel that the support offered may not be confidential (Kinman, Clements and Hart, 2015). However, some staff may feel that it is beneficial to be supported by someone who understands the job from the inside. Other Prison Service employees are well placed to have such insights. One solution in addressing such mixed needs is to give those involved in incidents, whether finding a body hanging or other major incidents, a choice of whether or not to have some of their support needs met by an external agency or internal arrangements.

It is clear from the above discussion that SIDs in prison can have a significant impact on family, prisoners and staff and there are some overlaps with their experiences. With regard to prison staff and the impacts of PTSD after a suicide in prison this area may very well benefit from further critical qualitative investigation. In the final section of this chapter we outline the procedural guidance that is currently in place for prison staff to follow when a death in custody occurs in England or Wales.

Procedures Following a Self-inflicted Death in Custody

During 2013, the Prison Service issued revised guidance and a PSI on procedures for the management of prisoners at-risk of harm to self, to others and from others (PSI 64/2011). This new framework sets out the expectations from NOMS for implementing safer custody procedures and practices to ensure that prisons are safe places for all those who live and work there. PSI 64/2011 replaced Prison Service Order (PSO) 2700 Suicide Prevention and Self-harm Management, PSO 2750 Violence Reduction, and PSO 2710 Follow Up to Deaths in Custody. Apart from generally drawing together good practice, the PSI aims to:

- Identify, manage and support prisoners and detainees who are at-risk of harm to self, others, and from others.
- Reduce incidents of self-harm and deaths in custody.
- Manage and reduce violence, deal effectively with perpetrators and support victims.
- Support effective multi-disciplinary case management and sharing of information to reduce incidents of harm.
- Ensure staff, prisoners and visitors affected by incidents of harm are supported appropriately
- Ensure appropriate responses and investigations to incidents, which promote learning to prevent future occurrences and improve local delivery of safer custody services.

Following a death in custody prison staff are also required to follow PSO 140 'Incident Management' alongside PSI 64/2001 to ensure all relevant stakeholders are informed. Mandatory actions for prison staff are highlighted throughout PSI 64/2011 (in italics). The instructions make it clear that, as in hospitals, a qualified medical doctor is the only person to be able to officially pronounce death. Prisons must have a nominated family liaison officer (FLO) and they are the named point of contact for the family. Their rôle is to maintain contact with the family, and provide information and practical support where appropriate. The Governor will also write a personal letter of condolence to the family, which will include an invitation to the family to visit the prison and an offer to contribute to funeral expenses.

In parallel with the coroner's independent judicial investigation the Prisons and Probation Ombudsman (PPO) investigates all deaths that occur in prisons and young offender institutions. The PPO is independent of NOMS (including HM Prison Service and Probation Services in England and Wales), the United Kingdom Border Agency and the Youth Justice Board (🌀 www.ppo.gov.uk). Since 1 April 2004 the PPO has undertaken this rôle and establishes the circumstances and events surrounding the death, particularly how the person who died was looked after while they were in custody (🌀 www.ppo.gov.uk). Once the investigation has been completed the PPO produces a report, explaining their findings, including whether the prison's actions were appropriate and any recommendations to prevent deaths in the future. Although the PPO recommendations are non-binding, prison staff do sometimes implement them.

Lastly, on 1 September 2011 there was an extension of the Corporate Manslaughter and Homicide Act 2007, which now includes custody providers, namely prisons, secure hospitals, police, immigration detention centres and juvenile detention facilities (🌀 iapdeathsincustody. independent.gov.uk). The prison Governor can therefore be convicted of a corporate manslaughter offence if an individual dies in their custody, and prosecutions can take place if it can be proved that the way the facilities are managed or organized caused a death and amounted to a breach of the duty of care. The penalty for the organizations convicted is a fine with no maximum limit (iapdeathsincustody.independent. gov.uk). The new extension on the Act was welcomed by families of those who die in custody as it would provide extra protection for vulnerable individuals and INQUEST believed that it would also inject some accountability into the system as that organization has revealed cases where there has been a catalogue of shortcomings in the treatment and care of vulnerable people in custody. It should also be noted that this extension of the Act also gives the Crown Prosecution Service the power and ability to prosecute individuals such as prison officers for individual gross negligence manslaughter. At the time of writing (mid-2015) there have been very few prosecutions for corporate manslaughter under the Act and the ones that have occurred have involved small, owner-managed companies and not prisons.

As highlighted in *Chapter 6,* prison staff have an important rôle to play in the prevention of self-injury and suicide but particularly following a SID in custody. There is therefore a need to provide potential approaches to support self-injury and suicide prevention frameworks. A key factor in an individual's response to challenging and difficult events is their level of resilience. Resilience is often defined as the ability to 'bounce back' from stressors and reinstate equilibrium within their life (Paton *et al,* 2008). Resilience training and its impact as well as effective working practice may be of relevance to those employed in the Prison Service, particularly after exposure to a suicide in prison. Attention will now be given to the notion of resilience, staff-prisoner relationships, self-injury and suicide.

Promoting Resilience in Prison Staff

It has been argued that having collective, reassuring, encouraging, non-judgemental and empathic prisoner-staff relationships are key factors for developing positive rehabilitative outcomes (e.g. Bennett and Shuker, 2010; Stevens, 2010). With regard to suicidality, having a positive therapeutic alliance is essential to the treatment and management of suicidal individuals, and an improved therapeutic relationship has been linked to better depression treatment outcomes (Sakinofsky, 2007; Klein *et al,* 2003). Further, the staff-client relationship is considered to be a critical factor in lessening the risk of suicide (Burgess *et al,* 2000). It would therefore appear that there is strong support for the preventative rôle of a good collaborative and empathic working relationship between staff and suicidal individuals.

Limited prison studies have been conducted in this area, however in 2013 the positive and negative effects of a range of experiences were investigated, but in particular the impact of encountering self-injury, suicide and related suicidal behaviour amongst prisoners on staff (Slade and Lopresti, 2013). Further, they investigated how the resilience of staff could be improved and effective working relationships between staff and prisoners maintained. Across six prisons in England, a total of 281 prison officer, custodial manager, governor and operational support grades completed a survey concerning their attitudes to suicide, their level of resilience, the type of emotional labour employed at work and the style of their working relationships with individual prisoners, centring upon prisoners who were suicidal.

The key conclusions from the research study were that prison staff experience challenging and problematic situations in their everyday working environment that has both positive and negative outcomes; for staff these can impact on their relationships in work, resilience levels and style of emotional labour. Staff expressed that effective working relationships and strong resilience were both supported and maintained through the 'hiding' or 'faking' of true feelings and emotions. The authors suggested that this hiding by staff about their true feelings might be used for three key reasons (partnership, prisoner confidence and prisoner openness) so that the prisoners engage with them and they can offer support. However, it was recognised that pretending or hiding emotions may be also detrimental for prison staff. Lastly, it was found that serious self-injury decreased a sense of bond or attachment between staff and prisoners, and witnessing suicide (fatal or near-fatal) initially increased the acceptance of suicide amongst staff. Some of the main recommendations from the findings were that staff may benefit from resilience training, mentoring or supervision systems to support and guide them; there should be greater support for experienced staff to maintain effective styles of emotional labour; and there should be additional training for staff working with prisoners at-risk of self-injury and suicide.

It would appear then that fostering the establishment of positive, collaborative and mutually respectful relationships with prisoners is very important, and it would seem that these relationships are required to support prisoners engaging in self-injury and suicide. The notions of 'resilience' and 'emotional labour' are therefore powerful concepts through which to view the working worlds of prison staff. Prisons are emotionally challenging and demanding environments and the feelings generated by custodial work are many and varied. However, they are rarely freely aired and communicated. From the limited research that has been undertaken, prison staff have an assortment of well-practised emotion-work approaches that appear to keep unwanted emotions in check so that they are not displayed to prisoners. Presently, it would seem that the current working conditions in prisons place significant psychological pressures on prison officers and as Crawley (2004) argues 'failure to display the right emotions is to risk the acquisition of a deviant identity—someone who is either not "one of us" or not "up to the job"' (p 26).

Chapter Summary Points

- In order to work with the aftermath of suicide, staff need to understand the concept and stages of the bereavement process. This will help them understand their own reactions and also potentially be more empathic with those who need support through what is often a difficult process.

- There are some particular issues associated with suicide bereavement and the term 'suicide survivor' has been used in the literature to describe those who have experienced the death of a loved one.

- It is the bereaved families and friends who need information and to be worked with in a supportive and thoughtful fashion in coming to terms with their loss—this does not appear to consistently happen and it needs to.

Future Directions

We believe that not only a wider dissemination of the concept of bereavement is needed but also a further exploration of the incidents of post-traumatic stress reactions or disorders too. If staff are to provide the best level of care to prisoners staff need care and support themselves especially in view of the increasingly challenging operating conditions of public service provision at a time of severe cutbacks in funding. One conclusion of the Harris Review with regard to SIDs was the need for appropriate financial resources if we are to reduce suicides.

Further Reading:

1. Dawes, J. (1999) Deaths in custody: Moving beyond a statistical analysis. Paper presented at the 3rd National Outlook Symposium on Crime in Australia, Mapping the Boundaries of Australia's Criminal Justice System convened by the Australian Institute of Criminology and held in Canberra, 22-23 March.

    This paper summarises some of the research undertaken in South Australia into the deaths of 38 prisoners (37 male and one female) in the South Australia adult prison system, which occurred from 1 January 1980 to 31 March 1993. It is argued that deaths in custody result from interaction of 'importation' factors (those personal characteristics and experiences brought with the prisoner to the custodial experience) and 'deprivational' factors, that is, those negative and unhelpful events experienced by the prisoner within the prison system.

2. Kinman, G., Clements, A. and Hart, J. (2015) Concerns over the lack of support for prison officers' mental health. Paper presented at the British Psychological Society's Division of Occupational Psychology Conference in Glasgow, 7-9 January.

This paper presents the findings of a national survey conducted with prison officers by a research team at the University of Bedfordshire in England. The survey consisted of 1,682 participants who were predominantly male (85 per cent) and had worked for the Prison Service for an average of 18 years. It found that officers regularly reported psychological health problems related to their working conditions, such as depression, anxiety and emotional exhaustion, as well as sleeping difficulties and cognitive deficits. Of particular concern was the finding that disclosing work-related stress was highly stigmatised in the Prison Service with little available support or training. The paper concludes that there are concerns about the effects of work-related stress on the health and safety of people working in both secure hospitals and prisons.

3. Snow, L. and McHugh, M (2002) The aftermath of a death in prison custody. In G. Towl, Snow, L. and McHugh, M., *Suicide in Prisons*. Oxford: Blackwell Publishers.

This chapter addresses some of the difficult and challenging areas associated with the aftermath of a suicide in prison. It examines the impact on the different groups who are likely to be affected, for example, family, friends, other prisoners, and staff. Attention is given to the notion of bereavement, the inquest procedure and the responsibilities of the prison services.

4. Wright, L., Borrill, J., Teers, R. and Cassidy, T. (2006) The mental health consequences of dealing with self-inflicted death in custody. *Counselling Psychology Quarterly*, 19(2): 165–180.

This article discusses the findings of the impact of dealing with a death in custody from a prison officer's perspective. The findings suggested that out of 49 prison officers who had dealt with such an event in the period three-seven months prior to the study, 36.7% identified that they had an incidence rate of post-traumatic stress disorder (PTSD). Optimism, avoidance problem-solving style, prior experience of suicide and level of involvement in the incident were direct mediators of the impact of the event for the total sample, while perceived control, emotional support and other aspect of problem-solving style had an indirect effect. Separate analysis of the PTSD and non-PTSD groups showed that the only mediator for the PTSD group was prior experience. For the non-PTSD group a range of variables mediated the impact.

Appendix

Table 1: Outline of the STORM training package

There are four modules:
- Assessment
- Crisis management
- Problem-solving
- Crisis intervention

Each module is flexible, and if necessary can be delivered in two hours.
Educational methods used in each training session:
1. Brief lectures on background knowledge and the skills to be acquired and rehearsed
2. Focused group discussion
3. Modelling using STORM videotape material demonstrating the skills being used by healthcare staff
4. Role-play (rehearsal of skills) in trios (staff-client-observer) using pre-prepared rôle-play scripts to facilitate the practice of specific micro-skills
5. Video-feedback in small group setting of recorded rôle-played interviews carried out by course participants

The material can be modified in content for:
- Primary care teams
- Mental healthcare staff
- Accident and emergency staff

References

Abel, K., Shaw, J., Walker, T., Roberts, C. and Murphy, C. (2015). *Women Offenders Repeat Self-harm Intervention Pilot II (WORSHIP II)*. National Institute for Health Research for Patient Benefit (RfPB) Programme Final Report Form.

Alexander, D., Klein, S., Gray, N., *et al* (2000). Suicide by patients: Questionnaire study of its effect on consultant psychiatrists. *British Medical Journal,* 320, 1571–1574.

American Psychiatric Association (APA) (2013). *Diagnostic and Statistical Manual of Mental Disorders* (5th ed., text rev.). Washington, DC: APA.

Appleby, L., Morriss, R., Gask, L., Roland, M., Lewis, B., Perry, A., Battersby, L., Colbert, N., Green, G., Amos, T., Davies, L. and Faragher, B. (2000). An educational intervention for front-line health professionals in the assessment and management of suicidal patients (The STORM Project). *Psychological Medicine.* 30 805–812.

Apter, A., Kotler, M., and Sevy, S. (1991). Correlates of risk of suicide in violent and nonviolent psychiatric patients. *American Journal of Psychiatry*, 148, 883–887.

Arnold, R. A. (1990). Processes of victimization and criminalization of black women. *Social Justice*, 17, 153–166.

Baldry, E. (2009). Punishing the vulnerable: Women with mental health disorders and cognitive disabilities in the NSW Criminal Justice System. Paper presented at the Sisters Inside Conference, Brisbane.

Baldwin, L. (2015). *Mothering Justice: Working with Mothers in Criminal and Social Justice Settings*. Hook: Waterside Press.

Barnish, M. (2004). *Domestic Violence: A Literature Review.* London: HM Inspectorate of Probation.

Bartlett, A. *et al.* (2014). *The Forensically Modified Dialectical Behavior Therapy (DBT) Options Programme Study Report.* St George's, University of London.

Bartlett, A., Walker, T., Harty, M.A. and Abel, K. (2014). Health and social care services for women offenders: Current provision and a future model of care. *Journal of Forensic Psychiatry and Psychology*, 25(6), 625–635.

Beck, A.T., Kovacs, M., and Weissman, A. (1979). Assessment of suicidal ideation: The scale for suicide ideation. *Journal of Consulting and Clinical Psychology*, 47, 343–352.

Beckett, C. (1999). Deaths in custody and the inquest system. *Critical Social Policy*, 19 (2), 271–80.

Bennett, P. and Shuker, R. (2010). Improving Prisoner-Staff Relationships: Exporting Grendon's Good Practice. *Howard Journal of Criminal Justice*, 49(5), 491–502.

Biggam, E. and Power, K. (1999). Social problem-solving skills and psychological distress among incarcerated young offenders, the issue of bullying and victimization. *Cognitive Therapy and Research*, 23: 307–26.

Bille-Brahe, U. and Jessen, G. (1994). Repeated suicidal behavior: A two-year follow-up. *Crisis*, 15, 77–82.

Bogue, J. and Power, K. 1995. Suicide in Scottish prisons, 1976–93. *Journal of Forensic Psychiatry*, 6: 527–40.

Blackburn, A., Mullings, J and Arquart, J. (2008). Sexual assault in prison and beyond: Lifetime sexual assault among incarcerated women. *Prison Journal*, 88, 3, 351–377.

Bloom, B., Owen, B. and Covington, S. (2003). *Gender-Responsive Strategies: Research, Practice, and Guiding Principles for Women Offenders*. Washington DC: US Department of Justice, National Institute of Corrections.

Bloom, B. and Covington, S. (2000). Gendered justice: Programming for women in correctional settings. Paper presented to the American Society of Criminology, San Francisco, CA.

Bonanno, G. A. (2004). Loss, trauma, and human resilience: Have we underestimated the human capacity to thrive after extremely aversive events? *American Psychologist*, 59, 20–28.

Borrill, J., Burnett, R., Atkins, R., Miller, S., Briggs, D., Weaver, T., and Maden, A. (2003). Patterns of self-harm and attempted suicide among whites and black/mixed race female prisoners. *Criminal Behaviour and Mental Health*, 13, 229–240.

Borrill. J., Snow, L., Medlicott, D., Teers, R. and Paton, J. (2005). Learning from near misses: Interviews with women who survived an incident of severe self-harm in prison. *Howard Journal*, 44 (1), 57–69.

Boudoukha, A.H., Przygodzki-Lionetb, N. and Hautekeeteb, M. (2011). Traumatic events and early maladaptive schemas (EMS): Prison guard psychological vulnerability. *Review of European Psychology*, in press.

Bowlby J. (1961). Processes of mourning. *International Journal of Psycho-Analysis*, 42: 317–340.

Bowlby, J. (1985). *Loss: Sadness and Depression.* Harmondsworth: Penguin.

Bowlby J. and Murray-Parkes C. (1970). Separation and loss within the family. In *The Child in His Family* (Anthony E. J. ed.) Whiley, New York, pp. 197–216.

Brady, K. (2001). Comorbid posttraumatic stress disorder and substance use disorders. *Psychiatric Annals.* 31, 313–9.

Brewer-Smyth, J. (2004). Women behind bars: Could neurobiological correlates of past physical and sexual abuse contribute to criminal behavior? *Health Care for Women International,* 25 (9), 835–852.

Briere, J. (1995). *Trauma Symptom Inventory: Professional Manual.* Florida, USA: Psychological Assessment Resources, Inc.

Brodsky, B. S., Groves, S. A., Oquendo, M. A., Mann, J. J., and Stanley, B. (2006). Interpersonal precipitants and suicide attempts in borderline personality disorder. *Suicide and Life Threatening Behaviors,* 36, 313–322. doi:10.1521/suli.2006.36.3.313

Browne, A., Miller, B., and Maguin, E. (1999). Prevalence and severity of lifetime physical and sexual victimization among incarcerated women. *International Journal of Law and Psychiatry,* 22, 301–322. doi:10.1016/S0160-2527(99)00011-4

Briere, J., and Gil, E. (1998). Self-mutilation in clinical and general population sample: Prevalence, correlates, and functions. *American Journal of Orthopsychiatry,* 68(4), 609–620.

Brown, M. Z., Comtois, K. A., and Linehan, M. M. (2002). Reasons for suicide attempts and nonsuicidal self-injury in women with borderline personality disorder. *Journal of Abnormal Psychology,* 111(1), 198–202.

Burgess, P., Pirkis, J., Morton, J. and Croke, E. (2000). Lessons from a comprehensive clinical audit of users of psychiatric services who committed suicide. *Psychiatric Services,* 51(12), 1555–1560.

Carlson, E. B., and Shafer, M. S. (2010). Traumatic histories and stressful life events of incarcerated parents: Childhood and adult trauma histories. *Prison Journal* 90, 4, 475–493.

Castille, K., Prout, M., Marczyk, G., Shmidheiser, M., Yoder, S., and Howlett, B. (2007). The early maladaptive schemas of self-mutilators: Implications for therapy. *Journal of Cognitive Psychotherapy,* 21(1), 58–71.

Chapman, A. L., Gratz, K. L., and Brown, M. (2006). Solving the puzzle of deliberate self-injury: The experiential avoidance model. *Behaviour Research and Therapy,* 44, 371–394.

Chapman, A. L., and Dixon-Gordon, K. L. (2007). Emotional antecedents and consequences of deliberate self-harm and suicide attempts. *Suicide & Life Threatening Behavior*, 37, 543–552. doi:10.1521/suli.2007.37.5.543

Chesney-Lind, M. and Rodriquez, N. (1983). Women under lock and key: A view from the inside. *Prison Journal*, 63, 47–65.

Chesney-Lind, M. (1998). The forgotten offender. *Corrections Today*, 60, 66–71.

Ciclitira, K., Adler, J., and Marzano, L. (2012). The impact of prison staff responses on self-harming behaviours: Prisoners' perspectives. *British Journal of Clinical Psychology*, 51(1), 4–18.

Clark, S., Lark, S. and Goldney, R. (1995). Grief reactions and recovery in a support group for people bereaved by suicide. *Crisis*, 16: 27–33.

Clark, S. and Goldney, R. (2000). The impact of suicide on relatives and friends. In *The International Handbook of Suicide and Attempted Suicide*. Chichester: John Wiley.

Corston, J. (2007). *The Corston Report: A Review of Women with Particular Vulnerabilities in the Criminal Justice System*. London: Home Office.

Covington, S., and Bloom. B. (2004). Creating gender-responsive services in correctional settings: Context and considerations. Paper presented at the American Society of Criminology Conference, Nashville, Texas.

Covington, S. and Bloom. B. (2006). Creating gender-responsive services in correctional settings: Context and considerations. Paper presented at the American Society of Criminology Conference, Nashville, Texas.

Covington, S. (2014). Creating gender-responsive and trauma-informed services for women in the justice system. *The Magistrate*, October/November 2014, Volume 70, Number 5, pp. 2–3. The Magistrates' Association: London, United Kingdom.

Cox, T. (1993). *Stress Research and Stress Management: Putting Theory to Work*. HSE Contract Research Report No 61: Sudbury.

Crawley, E.M. (2004). *Doing Prison Work: The Public and Private Lives*. Cullompton: Willian Publishing.

Crighton, D. (2000). Suicide in prisons in england and wales 1988–1998: An empirical study. PhD thesis submitted to Anglia Polytechnic University.

Crighton, D. (2006). Psychological research into reducing suicides. In Towl, G. (Ed.) *Psychological Research in Prisons*. Oxford: Wiley-Blackwell.

Crighton, D. (2012). Suicide, attempted suicide and self-injury in prisons. In Jones, P. (Eds.) *Interventions in Criminal Justice*. Hove: Pavilion Publishing and Media Ltd.

Crighton, D. and Towl, G. (1997). Self-inflicted deaths in England and Wales 1988–1990, and 1994–95, In *Suicide and Self-Injury in Prisons*, edited by G. Towl. Leicester: British Psychological Society.

Crighton, D. and Towl, G. (2002). Intentional self-injury. In Towl, G., Snow, L. and McHugh, M. (Eds.) *Suicide in Prisons*. Oxford: Blackwell.

Crighton, D. and Towl, G. (2008). *Psychology in Prisons*. 2nd edition. London: Wiley-Blackwell.

Crime and Misconduct Commission. (2007). *Breaking the Cycle: A Study of Victimisation and Violence in the Lives of Non-custodial Offenders*. Brisbane, Queensland, Australia: Crime and Misconduct Commission.

Criminal Justice Inspection Northern Ireland. (2009). *Prison Service Staff Training and Development*. Northern Ireland: Criminal Justice Inspection Northern Ireland.

Davies, R. (2004). New understandings of parental grief: Literature review. *Journal of Advanced Nursing, 46(5)*, 506–513.

Dawes, J. (1999). Deaths in custody: Moving beyond a statistical analysis. Paper presented at the 3rd National Outlook Symposium on Crime in Australia, Mapping the Boundaries of Australia's Criminal Justice System convened by the Australian Institute of Criminology held in Canberra, 22–23 March.

Dear, G. E., Thomson, D. M., and Hills, A. M. (2000). Self-harm in prisons: Manipulators can also be suicide attempters. *Criminal Justice and Behavior*, 27, 160–175. doi: 10.1177/0093854800027002002

Dear, G., Thomson, D., Howells, K. and Hall, G. (2001). Self-harm in western Australian prisons: Differences between prisoners who have self-harmed and those who have not. *Australian and New Zealand Journal of Criminology*, 34: 277–92.

DeHart, D. D. (2008). Pathways to prison: Impact of victimization in the lives of incarcerated women. *Violence Against Women*, 14, 1362–1381.

DeHart, D. D., Smith, H. P., and Kaminski, R. J. (2009). Institutional responses to self-injurious behavior among inmates. *Journal of Correctional Health Care*, 15, 129–141. doi:10.1177/1078345809331444

Department of Health. (1999). *The National Service Framework for Mental Health: Modern Standards and Service Models*. London: Department of Health.

Department of Health (2012). *Improving Outcomes and Supporting Transparency. Part 2: Summary Technical Specifications of Public Health Indicators*. London: Department of Health.

DeCatanzaro, D. (1981). *Suicide and Self-Damaging Behaviour. A Sociobiological Perspective.* New York: Academic Press.

DeHart, D. D. (2008). Pathways to prison: Impact of victimization in the lives of incarcerated women. *Violence Against Women*, 14, 1362–1381.

DeHart, D. D., Smith, H. P., and Kaminski, R. J. (2009). Institutional responses to self-injurious behavior among inmates. *Journal of Correctional Health Care*, 15, 129–141. doi:10.1177/1078345809331444.

Dirks, D. (2004). Sexual victimization and retraumatisation of women in prison. *Women Quarterley Studies*, 32, 3, 102–115.

Dixon-Gordon, K., Harrison, N., and Roesch, R.(2012). Non-suicidal self-injury within offender populations: A systematic review. *International Journal of Forensic Mental Health*, 11(1), 33–50.

Driessen, M., Schroeder, M., Bernhard, W., von Schinfeld, C and Schneider, M. (2006). Childhood trauma, psychiatric disorders and criminal behavior in prisoners in Germany: A comparative study in incarverated women and men. *Journal of Clinical Psychiatry*, 67, 1486–1492.

Dockley, A. (2008). Distressing times: What happens to vulnerable women when they come into custody. *Prison Service Journal.* webarchive.nationalarchives. gov.uk/20090215140630/http://www.hmprisonservice.gov.uk/resourcecentre/prisonservicejournal/index.asp?print=1&id=6159,3124,11,3148,0,0

Dooley, E. (1990). Non-natural deaths in prison. *British Journal of Criminology*, 30(2), 229–234.

Dulit, R. A., Fyer, M. R., Leon, A. C., Brodsky, B. S., and Frances, A. J. (1994). Clinical correlates of self-mutilation in borderline personality disorder. *American Journal of Psychiatry*, 151, 1305–1311.

Dockley, A. (2001). Suicide and self-harm prevention: Repetitive self-harm among women in prison. *Prison Service Journal*, 138, 27–29.

Duperouzel, H., and Fish, R. (2010). Hurting no-one else's body but your own: People with intellectual disability who self-injure in a forensic service. *Journal of Applied Research in Intellectual Disabilities*, 23, 606–615. doi:10.1111/j.1468-3148.2010.00559.x

Durcan, G. (2008). *From the Inside: Experiences of Prison Mental Health Care.* London: Centre for Mental Health.

Easteal, P. (2001).Women in Australian prisons: The cycle of abuse and dysfunctional environments. *Prison Journal*, 81, 87–112.

Evans, J., Williams, J., O'Loughlin, S. and Howells, K. (1992). Autobiographical memory and problem-solving strategies of parasuicide patients. *Psychological Medicine,* 22: 399–405.

Fazel S. and Danesh J. (2002). Serious mental disorders in 23 000 prisoners: A systematic review of 62 surveys. *Lancet,* 359, 545–50.

Favazza, A. R. (1998). The coming of age of self-mutilation. *The Journal of Nervous and Mental Disease,* 186(5), 259–268.

Feigelman, W., Gorman, B. and Jordan, J. (2009). Stigmatization and suicide bereavement. *Death Stud*ies, 33, 591–608

Fergus, L. and Keel, M. (2005). Conference Review: Is prison obsolete? *ACSSA Aware,* 9, 3–7. Melbourne: Australian Institute of Family Studies.

Finkelhor, D., Ormrod, R.K., Turner, H.A., and Hamby, S.L. (2005). Measuring poly-victimization using the JVQ. *Child Abuse & Neglect* 29, 11, 1297–1312.

Franklin, R. K. (1988). Deliberate self-harm: Self-injurious behavior within a correctional mental health population. *Criminal Justice and Behavior,* 15, 210–218. doi:10.1177/0 09385488015002007.

Freud S. (1961). Mourning and melancholia. In *The Standard Edition of the Complete Psychological Works of Sigmund Freud* (Strachey J. ed. and trans.), Hogarth Press, London (Original work published 1917), pp. 239–260.

Fulwiler, C., Forbes, C., Santangelo, S. L., and Folstein, M. (1997). Self-mutilation and suicide attempt: Distinguishing features in prisoners. *Journal of the American Academy of Psychiatry and the Law,* 25(1), 69–77.

Forrestor, A. and Slade, K. (2013). Preventing self-harm and suicide in prisoners: Job half done. *The Lancet,* ⟳ thelancet.com Published online September 16, 2013 ⟳ dx.doi.org/10.1016/S0140-6736(13)62571-4

Franklin, C.A. (2008). Women offenders, disparate treatment, and criminal justice: A theoretical, historical, and contemporary overview. *Criminal Justice Studies: A Critical Journal of Crime, Law and Society,* 21(4), 341–360.

Fredrickson, B., Tugade, M., Waugh, C. and Larkin, G. (2003). What good are positive emotions in crisis? A prospective study of resilience and emotions following the terrorist attacks on the United States on September 11th. *Journal of Personality and Social Psychology.* 84: 365–376.

Gardner, A. R., and Gardner, A. J. (1975). Self-mutilation, obsessionality, and narcissism. *British Journal of Psychiatry,* 127, 127–132. doi: 10.1192/bjp.127.2.127.

Gask, L. (1998). Small group interactive techniques utilizing video feedback. *International Journal of Psychiatry in Medicine* 28 (1), 97–113

Gask, L. and Morriss, R. (1996). *STORM Version One.* Manchester: University of Manchester.

Gask, L. and Lever-Green, G. (2003). *Prison STORM.* Manchester: University of Manchester.

Gask, L., Dixon, C., Morriss, R., Appleby, L. and Green, G. (2006). Evaluating STORM skills training for managing people at-risk of suicide. *Nursing and Healthcare Management and Policy.* 739–750.

Gee, J. and Reed, S., (2013). The HoST programme: A pilot evaluation of modified dialectical behaviour therapy with female offenders diagnosed with borderline personality disorder. *European Journal of Psychotherapy & Counselling*, 15(3), 233–252.

Gilfus, M. (1992). From victims to survivors to offenders: Women's routes of entry and immersion into street crime. *Women and Criminal Justice*, 4, 63–89.

Girshick, L. (1999). *No Safe Haven: Stories from Women in Prison.* New York: North Eastern University Press.

Gladstone, G. L., Parker, G. B., Mitchell, P. B., Malhi, G. S., Wilhelm, K., and Austin, M. (2004). Implications of childhood trauma for depressed women: An analysis of pathways from childhood sexual abuse to deliberate self-harm and revictimization. *American Journal of Psychiatry*, 161, 1417–1425.

Goff A, Rose E, Rose S, and Purves D. (2007). Does PTSD occur in sentenced prison populations? A systematic literature review. *Criminal Behaviour and Mental Health*, 17, 152–62.

Gray, N.S., Hill, C., McGleish, A., Timmons, D., MacCulloch, M.J., and Snowden, R.J. (2003). Prediction of violence and self-harm in mentally disordered offenders: A prospective study of the efficacy of HCR-20 , PCL-R, and psychiatric symptomatology. *Journal of Consulting and Clinical Psychology*, 71(3), 443–451.

Green, B. L., Miranda, J., Daroowalla, A., and Siddique, J. (2005). Trauma exposure, mental health functioning, and program needs of women in jail. *Crime and Delinquency*, 51, 133–151.

Goldson, B. and Coles, D. (2005). *In the Care of the State?* London: INQUEST.

Gough, K. (2005). Guidelines for managing self-harm in a forensic setting. *The British Journal of Forensic Practice*, 7, 10–14.

Grandey, A. (2000). Emotion regulation in the workplace. *Journal of Occupational Health Psychology.* 5 (1), 95–110.

Gratz, K. L. (2003). Risk factors for and functions of deliberate self-harm: A conceptual review. *Clinical Psychology Science and Practice*, 10, 192–205. doi:10.1093/clipsy.bpg022

Gratz, K. L. (2006). Risk factors for deliberate self-harm among female college students: The role and interaction of childhood maltreatment, emotional inexpressivity, and affect intensity/reactivity. *American Journal of Orthopsychiatry*, 76, 238–250.

Greenfeld, L. and Snell, T. (2000). *Bureau of Justice Statistics Special Report: Women Offenders.* Washington: US Department of Justice.

Grubin D, Carson D, Parsons S. (2002). *Report on New Prison Reception Health Screening Arrangements: The Results of a Pilot Study in Ten Prisons.* Newcastle upon Tyne. University of Newcastle.

Gunnell, D., Hawton, K. and Kapur, N. (2011). Coroners verdicts and suicide statistics in England and Wales. *British Medical Journal,* 343, 1–2.

Guthrie, E., Moorey, J., Margison, F., Barker, H., Palmer, S., McGrath, G., *et al.* (1999). Cost-effectiveness of brief psychodynamic-interpersonal therapy in high utilizers of psychiatric services. *Archives of General Psychiatry*, 56, 51926.

Guthrie, E., Kapur, N., Mackway-Jones, K., *et al* (2001). Randomised controlled trial of brief psychological intervention after deliberate self-poisoning. *British Medical Journal,* Volume 323, 1–4.

Haines, J. and Williams, C. L. (1997). Coping and problem-solving of self-mutilators. *Journal of Clinical Psychology*, 53, 177–186.

Hales L and Gelsthorpe L (2012). *The Criminalisation of Migrant Women,* Cambridge, UK: Institute of Criminology, University of Cambridge.

Hales, H., Freeman, M., Edmonson, A. and Taylor, P. (2014). Witnessing suicide-related behavior in prison: A qualitative study of young male prisoners in England. *Crisis.* 35(1), 10–7.

Hall, B., and Gabor, P. (2004). Peer suicide prevention in a prison. *Crisis*, 25, 19–26.

Hancock, N. and Graham, L. (2008). First-night centres. In Jewkes, Y. and Bennett, J. (Eds.) *Dictionary of Prisons and Punishment,* Cullompton: Willan.

Hannah-Moffat, K. (2000). Prisons that empower: Neo-liberal governance in canadian women's prisons. *British Journal of Criminology*, 4, 510–531.

Hansard, H. (2013). House of Commons written answers. 18 July: Column 854W.

Hanson, C. (2014). Prison officer training—An insight. *Inside Time: The National Newspaper for Prisoners and Detainees.*

Hawton, K. and Simkin, S. (2003). Helping people bereaved by suicide. *British Medical Journal*, 327: 177–178.

Harrick's, J., Price, S., House, A., *et al.* (2003). Self-injury attendances in the accident and emergency department: Clinical database study. *British Journal of Psychiatry*, 183: 34–39.

Harris Review. (2015). *Changing Prisons, Saving Lives: Report of the Independent Review into Self-inflicted Deaths in Custody of 18–24 year olds.* London, Cm 9087.

Harris, M., and Fallot, R. D. (2001). Envisioning a trauma-informed service system: A vital paradigm shift. *New Directions for Mental Health Services*, 89, 3–22.

Hasking, P., Momeni, R., and Swannell, S. (2008). The nature and extent of non-suicidal self-injury in a non-clinical sample of young adults. *Archives of Suicide Research*, 12, 208–218. doi:10.1080/13811110802100957

Hauser, M. (1987). Special aspects of grief after a suicide. In E. J. Dunne, J. L. McIntosh, and K. Dunne-Maxim (Eds.), *Suicide and its Aftermath: Understanding and Counseling the Survivors* (pp. 57–72). New York: Norton.

Haw, C., Hawton, K., Houston, K., and Townsend, E. (2001). Psychiatric and personality disorders in deliberate self-harm patients. *British Journal of Psychiatry*, 178, 48–54.

Hawton, K., Rodham, K., and Evans, E. (2002). Deliberate self-harm in adolescents: Self-report survey in schools in England. *British Medical Journal*, 325: 1207–1211.

Hawton, K., Linsell, L., Adeniji, T,. Sariaslan, S. and Fazel, S. (2013). Self-harm in prisons in England and Wales: An epidemiological study of prevalence, risk factors, clustering, and subsequent suicide. *The Lancet*, thelancet.com Published online September 16, 2013 dx.doi.org/10.1016/S0140-6736(13)62571-4.

Haycock, J. (1989). Manipulation and suicide attempts in jails and prisons. *Psychiatric Quarterly*, 60: 85–98.

Hayes, A. and Lever-Green, G. (2006). Developments in suicide prevention training for prison staff: STORM and beyond. *The Journal of Mental Health Training, Education and Practice.* 1(44) 23–28.

Hayes, A., Shaw, J. and Lever-Green, G. (2008). Improvements to suicide prevention training for prison staff in England and Wales. *Suicide and Life-Threatening Behavior* 38(6) 708–713.

Health and Care Professions Council. (2008). *Standards of Conduct, Performance and Ethics.* London: HCPC.

Herpertz, S., Sass, H., and Favazza, A. (1997). Impulsivity in self-mutilative behavior: Psychometric and biological findings. *Journal of Psychiatric Research*, 31, 451–465.

Hillbrand, M., Young, J. L., and Krystal, J. H. (1996). Recurrent self-injurious behavior in forensic patients. *Psychiatric Quarterly*, 67, 33–45.

HM Inspectorate of Prisons. (1986). *Working Group on Suicide Prevention,* London: Home Office.

HM Inspectorate of Prisons. (1990). *Review of Suicide and Self-Harm.* London: Home Office.

HM Inspectorate of Prisons. (1999). *Suicide is Everyone's Concern: A Thematic Review.* London: Home Office.

HM Inspectorate of Prisons (2007). *HMP Foston Hall: Not Yet Adapted to Changed Role.* London: Home Office.

HM Chief Inspector of Prisons. (1999). *Suicide is Everyone's Concern: A Thematic Review by HM Chief Inspector of Prisons for England and Wales.* London, UK: HMSO.

HM Chief Inspector of Prisons (2014). *Annual Report for England and Wales 2013–2014.* London: Home Office.

HM Prison Service. (1993). *Guide to Policies and Procedures — Caring for the Suicidal in Custody. Instructions to Governors,* 1/94. London, UK: Author.

HM Prison Service. (1994). *Caring for the Suicidal in Custody.* Instruction to Governors 1/ 94.

HM Prison Service. (2001). *Prevention of Suicide and Self-Harm in the Prison Service.* London, UK: Ministry of Justice.

HM Prison Service (2007). *The Mental Health of Prisoners.* London: Home Office.

Hobson, R.F. (1985). *Forms of Feeling.* London: Tavistock.

Hochschild, A. (1983). *The Managed Heart: Commercialisation of Human Feeling.* Berkeley: University of California Press.

Home Office. (1984). *Suicide in Prisons.* London: HMSO.

Home Office. (1991). *Custody, Care and Justice: The Way Ahead for the Prison Service in England and Wales.* London: Home Office.

Home Office Prison Service. 1999. *Anti-Bullying Strategy.* Prison Service Order no. 1702.

Hooper, C. (2003). *Abuse, Interventions and Women in Prison: A Literature Review.* London: Home Office.

Horrocks, J., Price, S., and House, A. (2003). Self-injury attendances in the accident and emergency department: Clinical database study. *British Journal of Psychiatry*, 183: 34–39.

House of Commons Justice Committee. (2009). *Role of the Prison Officer: Twelfth Report of Session 2008–09.* London: The Stationery Office Limited.

House of Commons (2012). *Reducing Re-offending: The 'What Works' Debate?* London: The Stationery Office Limited

House of Commons Justice Select Committee (2013). *Women Offenders: After the Corston Report,* 🔗 parliament.uk/documents/commons-committees/Justice/Women-offenders.pdf

House of Lords, House of Commons and Joint Committee on Human Rights (2004). *Deaths in Custody.* London: The Stationery Office.

Howard League for Penal Reform. (2001). *Suicide and Self-harm Prevention: Repetitive Self-Harm Among Women and Girls in Prison.* London: Howard League for Penal Reform.

Howard League for Penal Reform. (2003). *Suicide and Self-injury Prevention 2: Repetitive Self-Injury Among Women and Girls in Prison.* London: Howard League for Penal Reform.

Howard League for Penal Reform. (2005). *Briefing Paper on Prison Overcrowding and Suicide.* London: Howard League for Penal Reform.

Howard League for Penal Reform. (2009). *Turnkeys or Professionals?* London: Howard League for Penal Reform.

Howard League for Penal Reform. (2014). *Breaking point: Understaffing and overcrowding in prisons.* London: Howard League for Penal Reform.

HSCIC. (2012). Self-harm: Hospital admission rate per 100,000 population in North East almost triple the rate in London. Retrieved 14 November 2013. 🔗 hscic.gov.uk/article/2430/Self-harm-hospital-admission-rate-per-100000-population-in-North-East-almost-triple-the-rate-in-London

Humber, N., Hayes, A., Senior, J., Fahy, T. and Shaw, J. (2011). Identifying, monitoring and managing prisoners at risk of self-harm/suicide in England and Wales, *Journal of Forensic Psychiatry & Psychology*, 22: 22–51.

INQUEST (2013). *The Impact of INQUEST's Service on Families' Experiences: An Analysis 2010–2013.* London: INQUEST.

Ireland, J.L. (1999). Bullying behaviors amongst male and female prisoners: A study of young offenders and adults. *Aggressive Behavior*, 25: 162–78.

Ireland, J.L. (2001). Bullying among female prisoners: A brief review of research. In F. Columbus (Ed.) *Advances in Psychology Research. Vol. II.* New York, NY: Nova Science Publishers.

Ireland, J.L. (2002). *Bullying Among Prisoners: Evidence, Research and Intervention Strategies.* Hove: Brunner-Routledge.

Ireland, J. L., and Quinn, K. (2007). Officer attitudes towards adult male prisoners who self-harm: Development of an attitudinal measure and investigation of sex differences. *Aggressive Behavior, 33*, 63–72.

Ivanoff, A., and Hayes, L. M. (2001). Preventing, managing, and treating suicidal actions in high-risk offenders. In J. B. Ashford and B. Sales (Eds.), *Treating Offenders with Mental Disorders* (pp. 313–331). Washington, DC: American Psychological Association Press.

Jeglic, E. L., Vanderhoff, H. A., and Donovick, P. J. (2005). The function of self-harm behavior in a forensic population. *International Journal of Offender Therapy and Comparative Criminology, 49*, 131–142. doi: 10.1177/0306624×04271130

Jenkins, R. and Singh, B. (2000). General population strategies of suicide prevention. In Hawton, K. and van Heeringen, K. (Eds.). *The International Handbook of Suicide and Attempted Suicide.* New York: John Wiley and Sons Ltd.

Joiner, Jr., T. E., Conwell, Y., Fitzpatrick, K. K.,Witte, T. K., Schmidt, N. B., Berlin,M. T. and Rudd, M. D. (2005). Four studies on how past and current suicidality relate even when 'everything but the kitchen sink' is covaried. *Journal of Abnormal Psychology, 114*, 291–303.

Joyce, P. (2012). *Criminal Justice: An Introduction.* London: Routledge.

Junker, G., Beeler, A., and Bates, J. (2005). Using trained inmate observers for suicide watch in a federal correctional setting: A win-win solution. *Psychological Services, 2*, 20–27.

Jones, A. (1986). Self-mutilation in prison: A comparison of mutilators and nonmutilators. *Criminal Justice and Behavior, 13*(3), 286–296.

Jordan, J. (2001). Is suicide bereavement different? A reassessment of the literature. *Suicide Life Threatening Behavior, 31*, 91–102.

Jordan, J. (2008). Bereavement after suicide. *Psychiatric Annals, 38*: 679–685.

Kapur, N., House, A., Creed, F., *et al.* (1998). Management of deliberate self-poisoning in adults in four teaching hospitals. *British Medical Journal, 316*: 831–832.

Karp, J., Whitman, L. and Convit, A. (1991). Intentional ingestion of foreign objects by male prison inmates. *Hospital and Community Psychiatry, 42*: 533–535.

Kast, V. (1988). *A Time to Mourn: Growing through the Grief Process.* Trans. D. Dachler and F. Cairms. Einsiedeln, Switzerland: Daimon Verlag.

Kendall, K. (1993). *Program Evaluation of Therapeutic Services at the Prison for Women.* Ottawa: Correctional Service of Canada.

Kenning, C., Cooper, J., Short, V., Shaw, J., Abel, K. and Chew-Graham, C. (2010). Prison staff and women prisoner's views on self-injury; their implications for service delivery and development: A qualitative study. *Criminal Behaviour and Mental Health*, 20 (4), 274–284.

Kerkhof, A. and Blaauw, E. (2007). Suicide in prisons and remand centers: Screening and prevention. In D. Wasserman and C. Wasserman (Eds.), *The Oxford textbook on suicide: Continental perspectives.* London: The Oxford Press.

Kahn, W. (1993). Caring for the caregivers: Patterns of organizational caregiving. *Administrative Science Quarterly.* 38, 539–563.

Khantzian, E. (1985). The self-medication hypothesis of addictive disorders: Focus on heroin and cocaine dependence. *The American Journal of Psychiatry*, 142, 1259–64.

Kinderman, P. (2014). *A Prescription for Psychiatry.* London: Palgrave Macmillan.

Kinman, G., Clements, A. and Hart, J. (2015). Concerns over the lack of support for prison officers' mental health. Paper presented at the British Psychological Society's Division of Occupational Psychology Conference in Glasgow, 7–9 January.

Kirchner, T., Forns, M., and Mohino, S. (2008). Identifying the risk of deliberate self-harm among young prisoners by means of coping typologies. *Suicide and Life-Threatening Behavior*, 38, 42–48. doi:10.1521/suli.2008.38.4.442.

Klein, D., Schwartz, J., *et al.* (2003). Therapeutic alliance in depression treatment: Controlling for prior change and patient characteristics. *Journal of Consulting and Clinical Psychology*, 71(6), 997–1006.

Klonsky, E. D. (2008, November). Mechanisms for self-injurious behavior. Symposium presented at a meeting of the International Society for the Improvement and Teaching of Dialectical Behavior Therapy, Orlando, Florida, U.S.

Klonsky, E.D., Oltmanns, T.F., and Turkheimer, E. (2003). Deliberate self-harm in a nonclinical population: Prevalence and psychological correlates. *American Journal of Psychiatry*, 160(8), 1501–1508.

Klonsky, E.D., and Muehlenkamp, J.J. (2007). Self-injury: A research review for the practitioner. *Journal of Clinical Psychology: In Session*, 63, 1045–1056.

Konrad, N., Daigle, M.S., Daniel, A.E., Dear, G.E., Frottier, P., Hayes, L.M., Hayes LM, Kerkhof A, Liebling A. and Sarchiapone, M. (2007). Preventing suicide in prisons, Part 1: Recommendations from the international association for suicide prevention task force on suicide in prisons. *Crisis*, 28, 113–121.

Kreitman, N. (1977). *Parasuicide*. Chichester: Wiley.

Kruml, S. (1999). The heart working: An empirical investigation of the dimensions, antecedents, and outcomes of emotion labour. Doctoral dissertation, Temple University. *Dissertation Abstracts International*, 61, 261.

Kruml, S. and Geddes, D. (2000). Exploring the dimensions of emotional labour: The heart of Hochschild's work. *Management Communication Quarterly*. 14, 8–49.

Kubler-Ross, E. (1970). *On Death and Dying*. Tavistock: London.

Lancaster, D. (2001). Suicide and self-harm among women and girls in HMP Holloway. *Prison Service Journal*, 138: 19–21.

Leddy, J. and O'Connell, M. (2002). The prevalence, nature and psychological correlates of bullying in Irish prisons. *Legal and Criminological Psychology*, 7: 131–40.

Leibenluft, E., Green, S. and Giese, A. (1988). Mourning and milieu: Staff reaction to the death of an inpatient. *Psychiatric Hospital*, 19, 169–173.

Lever-Green, G. (2007). *STORM Version Two*. Manchester: University of Manchester.

Liebling, A. (1992). *Studies in Prison*. London: Routledge.

Liebling, A. (1994). Suicide among women prisoners. *Howard Journal*, 33 (1), 1–9.

Liebling, A. (2006). The role of the prison environment in prison suicide and prisoner distress. In Dear, G. *Preventing Suicide and Other Self-injury in Prison*. Basingstoke: Palgrave-Macmillan.

Liebling, A. (2007). Prison Suicide and its Prevention. In Jewkes, Y. (Ed.) *Handbook on Prisons*, Cullompton: Willan.

Liebling, A. and Krarup, H. (1993). *Suicide Attempts in Male Prisons*. London: Home Office.

Liebling, A. Durie, L. A., Van den Beuckel, A., Harvey, J., and Tait, S. (2003). Emerging findings from the first stages of the evaluation of the Safer Locals Programme. Paper presented to the Safer Custody Group, HM Prison Service Conference, July.

Liebling, A., Price, D. and Shefer, G. (2011). *The Prison Officer*, 2nd edition. Devon: Willan Publishing.

Lilley, R., Owens, D. and Horrocks, J. (2008). Methods of self-injury: A multicentre comparison of episodes of poisoning and injury. *British Journal of Psychiatry*, 192: 440–445.

Linehan, M. M. (1993). *Cognitive-Behavioural Treatment of Borderline Personality Disorder*. New York: Guilford Press.

Linehan, M., Schmidt, H., Dimeff, L., Craft, J., Kanter, J. and Comtois, K. (1999). Dialectical behavior therapy for patients with borderline personality disorder and drug-dependence. *American Journal of Addiction*, 8 (4), 279–292.

Little JD. (1992). Staff response to in-patient and out-patient suicide: What happened and what do we do? *Australian New Zealand Journal of Psychiatry.* 26, 162–167.

Lohner, J., and Konrad, N. (2006). Deliberate self-harm and suicide attempt in custody: Distinguishing features in male inmates' self-injurious behavior. *International Journal of Law and Psychiatry*, 29, 370–385. doi: 10.1080/17449200701321654

Lloyd, C. (1990). *Suicide and Self-Injury in Prison: A Literature Review,* London: Home Office.

Lloyd, E. E., Kelley, M. L., and Hope, T. (1997, April). Self-mutilation in a community sample of adolescents: Descriptive characteristics and provisional prevalence rates. Poster session presented at the annual meeting of the Society for Behavioral Medicine, New Orleans, LA.

Loucks, N. (1998). HMPI Corton Vale: Research into drugs and alcohol, violence and bullying, suicides and self-injury, and backgrounds of abuse. Scottish Prison Service Occasional Papers: 1/98.

Loucks, N. (2002). *Just Visiting? A Review of the Role of Prison Visitors' Centres.* London: Federation of Prisoners' Families Support Groups and the Prison Reform Trust.

Lynch, S. M., Fritch, A. M. and Heath, N. M. (2012). Looking beneath the surface: The nature of incarcerated women's experiences of interpersonal violence, mental health, and treatment needs. *Feminist Criminology*, 7, 4, 381–400.

Mackay, C., Cousins, R., Kelly, P. J., Lee, S. and McCaig, R. H. (2004). Management standards and work-related stress in the UK: Policy background and science. *Work and Stress*, 18: 91–112.

Macleod, A., Rose, G. and Williams, J. (1993). Components of hopelessness about the future in parasuicide. *Cognitive Therapy Research,* 17: 441–5.

Maden, A., Chamberlain, S., and Gunn, J. (2000). Deliberate self-harm in sentenced male prisoners in England and Wales: Some ethnic factors. *Criminal Behaviour and Mental Health*, 10, 199–204

Mangnall and Yurkovich (2010). A grounded theory exploration of deliberate self-harm in incarcerated women. *Journal of Forensic Nursing*, 6, 88–95. doi:10.1111/j.1939-3938.2010.01072.x.

Mannion, A. (2009). Self-harm in a dangerous and severely personality disordered population. *Journal of Forensic Psychiatry and Psychology*, 20, 322–331. doi:10.1080/14789940802377106.

Marcus-Mendoza, S., Klein-Saffron, J. and Lutze, F. (1998). A feminist examination of boot camp prison programs for women. *Women and Therapy*, 21, 173–185.

Marzano, L., and Adler, J. R. (2007). Supporting staff working with prisoners who self-harm: A survey of support staff dealing with self-harm in prisons in England and Wales. *International Journal of Prisoner Health*, 3, 268–282.

Marzano, L., Fazel, S., Rivlin, A., and Hawton, K. (2010). Psychiatric disorders in women prisoners who have engaged in near-lethal self-harm: Case-control study. *British Journal of Psychiatry*, 197, 219–226. doi: 10.1192/bjp.bp.109.075424.

McHugh, M. and Snow, L. (2000). Suicide Prevention: Policy and Practice. In Towl, G., Snow, L. and McHugh, M. (Eds.) *Suicide in Prisons*. Leicester: British Psychological Society.

McHugh, M. and Towl, G. (1997). Organisational Reactions and Reflections on Suicide and Self-Injury. In G. Towl. (Ed.) *Suicide and Self-injury in Prisons, Issues in Criminological and Legal Psychology*, 28. Leicester: British Psychological Society.

McIntosh, J. and Kelly, L. (1992). Survivors' reactions: Suicide vs. other causes. *Crisis*, 13: 82–93.

McQuaid, S. and Ehrenreich, J. (1998). Women in prison: Approaches to understanding the lives of a forgotten population. *Affiliated Journal of Women and Social Work*, 13, 233–246.

Meltzer, H., Harrington, R. and Goodman, R. (2001). *Children and Adolescents Who Try to Harm, Hurt or Kill Themselves: A Report of Further Analysis from the National Survey of the Mental Health of Children and Adolescents in Great Britain in 1999.* London: Office for National Statistics.

Meltzner, J. and Hayes, L. (2006). Suicide prevention in jails and prisons. In Simon, R. and Hales, R. *Textbook of Suicide Assessment and Management*. Washington: American Psychiatric Publishing.

Messina, N. and Grella, C. (2006). Childhood trauma and women's health outcomes in a California prison population. *American Journal of Public Health*, 96, 1842–8.

Miller, S., and Fritzon, K. (2007). Functional consistency across two behavioural modalities: Fire-setting and self-harm in female special hospital patients. *Criminal Behaviour and Mental Health*, 17, 31–44. doi:10.1002/cbm.637.

Milligan, R.J., and Andrews, B. (2005). Suicidal and other self-harming behaviour in offender women: The role of shame, anger and childhood abuse. *Legal and Criminological Psychology*, 10, 13–25.

Miller, S., and Fritzon, K. (2007). Functional consistency across two behavioural modalities: Fire-setting and self-harm in female special hospital patients. *Criminal Behaviour and Mental Health*, *17*, 31–44. doi: 10.1002/cbm.637.

Ministry of Justice. (2008). *Review of the Forum for Preventing Deaths in Custody.* London: Ministry of Justice Statistics Bulletin.

Ministry of Justice (2009). *Short Study on Women Offenders.* Social Exclusion Task Force. London: Cabinet Office.

Ministry of Justice. (2010). *National Service Framework: Improving Services to Women Offenders.* London: Ministry of Justice.

Ministry of Justice (2010b) *Statistics on Women and the Criminal Justice System.* London: Ministry of Justice.

Ministry of Justice. (2011). *Safety in Custody.* London: Ministry of Justice Statistics Bulletin.

Ministry of Justice. (2013). *Safety in Custody Statistics: Deaths in Prison Custody 1978–2012.* www.gov.uk/government/uploads/system/uploads/attachment_data/file/192434/safety-custody-deaths-dec-12.xls.

Ministry of Justice (2013b) *Safety in Custody Statistics England and Wales* Update to June 2013. London: Ministry of Justice.

Ministry of Justice (2013c) *Transforming Rehabilitation.* London: Ministry of Justice.

Ministry of Justice (2014). *Monthly Population Bulletin March 2014*, London: Ministry of Justice

Ministry of Justice (2015). *Self-Inflicted Deaths in Prison Custody in England and Wales Between 1978 and March 2014.* London: Ministry of Justice.

Ministry of Justice (2015b) *Safety in Custody Statistics England and Wales Deaths in Prison Custody to June 2015 Assaults and Self-harm to March 2015.* London: Ministry of Justice.

Moloney, K., Van den Bergh, B. and Moller, L. (2009). Women in prison: The central issues of gender characteristics and trauma history. *Public Health,* 123 426–430.

Morgan, H. (1979). *Death Wishes? The Understanding and Management of Deliberate Self-harm.* New York: John Wiley and Sons.

Morris. A. and Wilkinson, C. (1995). Responding to female prisoners' needs. *Prison Journal,* 75, 295–305.

Morriss, R., Gask, L., Battersby, L., Francheschini, A. and Robson, M. (1999). Teaching front-line health and voluntary workers to assess and manage suicidal patients. *Journal of Affective Disorders.* 52 77–83.

Morriss, R., Gask, L., Webb, R., Dixon, C., and Appleby, L. (2005). The effects on suicide of an educational intervention for front-line health professionals with suicidal patients (the STORM project). *Psychological Medicine*, 35, 957–960.

Mouzos J. and Makkai T. (2004). Childhood victimisation and the cycle of violence. In *Women's Experiences of Male Violence: Findings from the Australian Component of the International Violence Against Women Survey.* Canberra: Australian Institute of Criminology.

Muehlenkamp, J. J. (2006). Empirically supported treatments and general therapy guidelines for non-suicidal self-injury. *Journal of Mental Health Counseling*, 28(2), 166–180.

Murphy, S., Johnson, L., Chung, I. and Beaton, R. (2003). The prevalence of PTSD following the violent death of a child and predictors of change five years later. *Journal of Trauma Stress.* 16, 17–25.

Murray-Parkes C. (2001). Bereavement. *Oxford Textbook on Palliative Medicine.* Oxford: Oxford University Press.

National Bereavement Consortium (2001). *Bereavement Care Standards. UK Project.*

National Careers Service (2015). *Prison Officer.* nationalcareersservice.direct.gov.uk/advice/planning/jobprofiles/Pages/prisonofficer.aspx [25 May 2015].

Neville, K. and Roan, N. (2013). Suicide in Hospitalized Medical-Surgical Patients: Exploring Nurses' Attitudes. *Journal of Psychosocial Nursing and Mental Health Services.* 51(1), 35–43.

Newman, M., Guy, M., and Mastracci, S. (2008). Beyond cognition: Affective leadership and emotional labor, *Public Administration Review*, 69 (1), 6–20.

NOMS Learning and Development Group (2015). Personal communication on current staff training for prison officers. Walker, T. May 20 2015.

NICE. (2012). *Self-injury: Longer Term Management.* London: British Psychological Society and The Royal College of Psychiatrists.

Nock, M. K., and Prinstein, M. J. (2004). A functional approach to the assessment of self-mutilative behavior. *Journal of Consulting and Clinical Psychology*, 72, 885–890.

Nock, M. K., Prinstein, M. J., and Sterba, S. K. (2010). Revealing the form and function of self-injurious thoughts and behaviors: A real-time ecological assessment study among adolescents and young adults. *Journal of Abnormal Psychology*, 118, 816–827. doi: 10.1037/a0016948

O'Brien, M., Mortimer, L., Singleton, N., and Meltzer, H. (2003). Psychiatric morbidity among women prisoners in England and Wales. *International Review of Psychiatry*, 15, 153–157.

O'Connor, R. and Nock, M. (2014). The psychology of suicidal behaviour. *The Lancet Psychiatry*, 1, 73–85.

Ozer, E., Best, S., Lipsey, T. and Weiss, D. (2003). Predictors of posttraumatic stress disorder and symptoms in adults: A meta-analysis. *Psychological Bulletin*, 129: 52–71.

Paton, D. (1994). Disaster relief work: An assessment of training effectiveness. *Journal of Traumatic Stress.* 7, 275–288.

Paton, D. (2006). Post-traumatic growth in emergency professionals. In L. Calhoun and R Tedeschi. *Handbook Posttraumatic Growth: Research and Practice.* Mahwah, N: Lawrence Erlbaum.

Paton, D., Violanti, J.M. and Smith, L.M. (2003). *Promoting Capabilities to Manage Post-Traumatic Stress: Perspectives on Resilience.* Springfield, IL: Charles Thomas.

Paton, J. and Jenkins, R. 2005. Suicide and suicide attempts in prisons. In *Prevention and Treatment of Suicidal Behaviour: From Science to Practice*, K. Hawton. Oxford: University Press.

Paton, D., Violanti, J.M., Johnston, P., Burke, K.J., Clarke, J.M. and Keenan, D (2008). Stress Shield: A model of police resiliency, *International Journal of Emergency Mental Health*, 10(2),95–107.

Pattison, E. and Kahan, J. (1983). The deliberate self-harm syndrome. *American Journal of Psychiatry*, 140: 867–72.

Paul, T., Schroeter, K.,Dahme, B. and Nutzinger, D. (2002). Self-injurious behavior in women with eating disorders. *American Journal of Psychiatry*, 159, 408–411.

Paulus, P. B., and Dzindolet, M. T. (1993). Reactions of male and female inmates to prison confinement: Further evidence for a two-component model. *Criminal Justice and Behavior*, 20, 149–166. doi:10.1177/0093854893020002003.

Penfold, C., Turnbull, P. J., and Webster, R. (2005). *Tackling Prison Drug Markets: An Exploratory Qualitative Study.* London: Home Office.

Pengelly, N., Ford,B., Blenkiron, P.,and Reilly, S. (2008). Harm-minimization after repeated self-harm: Development of a trust handbook. *Psychiatric Bulletin*, 32, 60–63.

Pereira, C. (2001). Strip-searching as sexual assault. *Hecate*, 27, 187–196.

Plugge, E., Douglas, N., and Fitzpatrick, R. (2006). *The Health of Women in Prison: Study Findings*. UK: Department of Public Health, University of Oxford.

Pollock, J. M. (1998). *Counseling Women in Prison* (Vol. 3). Thousand Oaks: Sage Publications.

Pollock, S., and Brezina, K. (2006). Negotiating contradictions: Sexual abuse counseling with imprisoned women. In E. Leeder (Ed.), *Inside and Out: Women, Prison and Therapy*. New York: The Hawthorn Press, Inc.

Power, K. and Spencer, A. (1987). Parasuicidal behaviour of detained Scottish young offenders. *International Journal of Offender Therapy and Comparative Criminology*, 31: 227–35.

Powis, B. (2002). *Offenders' Risk of Serious Harm: A Literature Review*. London: Home Office Research, Development and Statistics Directorate.

Pratt, D., Piper, M., Appleby, L., and Shaw, J. (2006). Suicide in recently released prisoners: A population-based cohort study. *Lancet*, 368, 119–123.

Prinstein, M.J., Nock, M. K., Simon, V., Aikins, J.W., Cheah, C.S.L. and Spirito, A. (2008). Longitudinal trajectories and predictors of adolescent suicidal ideation and attempts following inpatient hospitalization. *Journal of Consulting and Clinical Psychology*, 76, 92–103.

Prison Service Order. (2003). Suicide and Self-harm Prevention. London: The Home Office.

Prison Disturbances. (1990). *Report of an Inquiry*. Paragraph 12.1 (Aka Woolf Inquiry. 🜨 discovery.nationalarchives.gov.uk/details/r/C9234).

Prisons and Probation Ombudsman. (2011). *Learning from PPO Investigations: Violence Reduction, Bullying and Safety*. London: Home Office.

Prison Service Instruction (2004). *Prison Service Training Policy*. London: Ministry of Justice.

Prison Service Order 4800. (2008). Women Prisoners. 🜨 www.justice.gov.uk/offenders/types-of-offender/women

Pugliesi, K. (1999). The consequences of emotional labour: Effects on work stress, job satisfaction, and well-being. *Motivation and Emotion*. 23 (2), 125–154.

Quina, K. and Brown, L. (2007). Introduction. *Journal of Trauma & Dissociation*, 8, 1–7.

Remer, P. (2003). Empowerment feminist therapy. Paper presented at the American Psychological Association Conference, August, 7–10.

Revolving Doors Agency (2002). *Bad Girls?: Women, Mental Health and Crime*. London: Revolving Doors

Rickford, D. (2003). *Troubled Inside: Responding to the Mental Health Needs of Women in Prison*. Prison Reform Trust. London: Prison Reform Trust

Rickford, D. and Edgar, K. (2005). *Troubled Inside: Responding to the Mental Health Needs of Men in Prison*, London: Prison Reform Trust.

Rieger, W. (1971). Suicide attempts in a federal prison. *Archives of General Psychiatry*, 24: 532–535.

Robinson, C. (2013). *Women's Custodial Estate Review*. London: National Offender Management Service.

Roe-Sepowitz, D. (2007). Characteristics and predictors of self-mutilation: A study of incarcerated women. *Criminal Behaviour and Mental Health*, 17, 312–321. doi: 10.1002/cbm.66

Rogers, P., Mitchell, D., Curran, J., Duggan, S. and Gournay, K. (2003). Post-traumatic stress disorder among prisoners. *Prison Service Journal*, 146: 24–30.

Royal College of Nursing. (2010). *Prison Mental Health: Vision and Reality*. London: Royal College of Nursing.

Royal College of Psychiatrists. (2002). *Suicide in Prisons*. London: Royal College of Psychiatrists.

Royal College of Psychiatrists. (2010). *Self-injury, Suicide and Risk: Helping People Who Self-harm*. London: Royal College of Psychiatrists.

Rumgay, J. (2004). *When Victims Become Offenders: In Search of Coherence in Policy and Practice*. London: Fawcett Society.

Sakinofsky, I. (2007). Treating suicidality in depressive illness. Part I: Current controversies. *Canadian Journal of Psychiatry*, 52, Supplement 1, 71–84.

Schwartz, R. H., Cohen, P., Hoffmann, N. G., and Meeks, J. E. (1989). Self-harm behaviors (carving) in female adolescent drug abusers. *Clinical Pediatrics*, 28, 340–346. doi:10.1177/000992288902800801

Seguin, M. L. (1995). Parental bereavement after suicide and accident: A comparative study. *Suicide and Life-Threatening Behaviour*, 25, 4: , 489–98.

Senior, J., Pratt, D., Shaw, J., *et al.* (2002). *An Evaluation of the F2052SH System for the Management of Suicide and Self-Harm Risk in Five Prisons*. London: Report to Safer Custody Group.

Shapiro, D., Barkham, M., Rees, A., Hardy, G., Reynolds, S. and Startup, M. (1994). Effects of treatment duration and severity of depression on the effectiveness of cognitive-behavioral therapy and psychodynamic-interpersonal psychotherapy. *Journal of Consulting and Clinical Psychology*, 62, 5228.

Shapiro, D., Rees, A., and Barkham, M. (1995). Effects of treatment duration and severity of depression on the maintenance of gains following cognitive behavioral therapy and psychodynamic-interpersonal psychotherapy. *Journal of Consulting and Clinical Psychology*, 63, 37887.

Shaw, J., Appleby, L. and Baker, D. (2003). *Safer Prisons—A National Study of Prison Suicides 1999–2000 by the National Confidential Inquiry into Suicide and Homicide by People with Mental Illness.* London: Department of Health.

Shaw, J., Baker, D., Hunt, I., Moloney, A. and Appleby, L. (2004). Suicide by prisoners: National clinical survey. *British Journal of Psychiatry*, 184: 263–267.

Shaw, J., Senior, J., Hayes, A., Davies, L., Appleby, L., Rogers, A., Bowen, A., Humber, N., Ogilvie, C., Daley, A., Train, L., Choudry, A., Ward,A., Lyndon, A., Foster, K., Clayton, R., Harrop, C., Da Cruz, D., Fahy, T., Thornicroft, G., Gournay, K., Thomas, S., Wright, S., Gillard, M., Birtles, C., Nafees, B., Lye, K. and Maden, T. (2006). *Evaluation of the 'Care of At Risk Prisoners Project'.* Report to Safer Custody Group. London: HMPS.

Shaw, J. and Turnbull, P. (2009). Suicide in custody, *Psychiatry,* 8: 265–268.

Shneidman, E. (1982). *Voices of Death: Personal Documents from People Facing Death.* New York: Bantam Books.

Shneidman, E. (1985). *Definition of Suicide.* New York: John Wiley and Sons.

Short, V., Cooper, J., Shaw, J., Kenning, C., Abel, K. and Chew-Graham, C. (2009). Custody vs. care: Attitudes of prison staff to self-harm in women prisoners-a qualitative study. *Journal of Forensic Psychiatry & Psychology*, 20, 408–426.

Silbert, M. and Pines, A. (1981). Sexual child abuse as an antecedent to prostitution. *Child Abuse and Neglect*, 5, 407–411.

Silverman, E. (1994). Bereavement from suicide as compared with other forms of bereavement. *Omega,* 30 (1), 41–51.

Skegg, K. (2005). Self-harm. *The Lancet*, 366, 1471–1483.

Slade, N. and Lopresti, S. (2013). *Promoting Resilience in Prison Staff.* London: Ministry of Justice.

Smith, R. (1984). Deaths in Prison. *British Medical Journal,* 288: 208–212

Smolin, A. and Guinan, J. (1993). *Healing After the Suicide of a Loved One.* New York: Simon & Schuster.

Snow, L. (1997). A pilot study of self-injury amongst women prisoners. *Issues in Criminological and Legal Psychology*, 28, 50–59.

Snow, L. (2002). Prisoners' motives for self-injury and attempted suicide. *British Journal of Forensic Practice*, 4, 18–29. doi:10.1108/14636646200200023

Snow, L. and McHugh, M (2002). The aftermath of a death in prison custody. In G. Towl, Snow, L. and McHugh, M. *Suicide in Prisons*. Oxford: Blackwell Publishers.

Social Exclusion Task Force. (2009). *Short Study on Women Offenders*. London: Cabinet Office and Ministry of Justice.

Speed, C. (2012). *Self-Inflicted Deaths in Prison: An Exploration of INQUEST's Challenges to State Power*. London: INQUEST.

Sprang, G. and McNeil, J. (1995). *The Many Faces of Bereavement: The Nature and Treatment of Natural, Traumatic, and Stigmatized Grief*. New York: Brunner/Mazel.

Stathopoulos, M. (2012). Addressing women's victimization histories in custodial settings. *ACSSA Issues*. Melbourne: Australian Institute of Family Studies.

Stevens, A. (2010). Introducing prison-based democratic therapeutic communities therapy. In R. Shuker and E. Sullivan (Eds.), *Grendon and the Emergence of Forensic Therapeutic Communities: Developments in Research and Practice*, Chichester: Wiley-Blackwell.

Strauser, D. and Lustig, D. (2001). The implications of post-traumatic stress disorder on vocational behaviour and rehabilitation planning. *Journal of Rehabilitation*, 67, 26–30.

Stroebe, W. and Stroebe, M. (1997). Determinants of adjustment to bereavement in younger widows and widowers. In *Handbook of Bereavement: Theory, Research, and Intervention* (Stroebe, M., Stroebe W. and Hansson R. (eds), Cambridge: Cambridge University Press, pp. 208–239.

Sutton, J. (2007). *Healing the Hurt Within: Understand Self-injury and Self-harm, and Heal the Emotional Wounds* (revised and updated 3rd edition). Oxford: How To Books.

Suyemoto, K. L. (1998). The functions of self-mutilation. *Clinical Psychology Review*, 18, 531–554.

Task Force on Suicide in Canada. (1994). *Suicide in Canada*. Ottawa: Minister of National Health and Welfare.

The Stationary Office (2006). *The Zahid Mubarek Inquiry*. London.

Towl, G. (1997). *Suicide and Self-Injury in Prisons, Issues in Criminological and Legal Psychology*, 28. Leicester: British Psychological Society.

Towl, G. (2000). Reflections upon suicide in prisons. *British Journal of Forensic Practice*, 2: 28–33.

Towl, G. (2010). Foreword in Harvey, J. and Smedley, K. (Eds.) *Psychological Therapy in Prisons and Other Secure Settings*. London: Willan Publishing.

Towl, G. (2015). Research informed practice into suicide in prisons: Ways forward in England and Wales, International Academy of Law and Mental Health 34th Conference, Vienna, 12th–17th July.

Towl, G., Snow, L. and McHugh, M. (2000). *Suicide in Prisons*. Plymouth: British Psychological Society.

Towl, G. and Hudson, D. (1997). Risk assessment and management. In Towl, G. (Ed.) *Suicide and Self-Injury in Prisons*. Leicester: British Psychological Society.

Towl, G. and Forbes, D. (2002). Working with suicidal prisoners. In Towl, G., Snow, L. and McHugh, M. (Eds.) *Suicide in Prisons*. Leicester: British Psychological Society.

Towl, G. and Crighton, D. (1998). Suicide in prisons in England and Wales from 1988 to 1995. *Criminal Behaviour and Mental Health*, 8: 184–192.

Towl, G. and Crighton, D. (2002). Editorial, *British Journal of Forensic Practice*, Vol. 4 Iss: 2, pp.2–2.

Towl, G. and Walker, T (2015). Prisoner Suicide. *The Psychologist*, 2–5.

Triplett, R., Mullings, J. L. and Scarborough, K. E. (1996). Work-related stress and coping among correctional officers: Implications from organizational literature. *Journal of Criminal Justice*, 24: 291–308.

Turner, H. A., Finkelhor, D., and Ormrod, R. K. (2006). The effect of lifetime victimization on the mental health of children and adolescents. *Social Science & Medicine*, 62(1), 13–27.

Van der Kolk, B., Perry, J., and Herman, J. (1991). Childhood origins of self-destructive behavior. *American Journal of Psychiatry*, 148, 1665–1671.

Walker, T. (2015). Self-injury and Suicide, in Towl, G. and Crighton, D. (Eds.) *Forensic Psychology*. London: Wiley-Blackwell.

Walker, T., Shaw, J., Turpin, C., Roberts, C. Murphy, C. and Abel, K. (2015). Goodbye letters in prison therapy: A qualitative analysis of self-harming women prisoner's experiences in England. In preparation for *Crisis*.

Walker, T., Shaw, J., Roberts, C. Murphy, C. and Abel, K., (2015). Attitudes of imprisoned women and prison staff to self-injury: A qualitative study. In preparation.

Walsh, B. and Rosen, P. (1988). *Self-Mutilation: Theory, Research and Treatment*. New York: Guilford Press.

Walter, T. (1994). *The Revival of Death*. London: Routledge.

Welch, S. S., and Linehan, M. M. (2002). High-risk situations associated with parasuicide and drug use in borderline personality disorder. *Journal of Personality Disorders*, 16, 561–569. doi:10.1521/pedi.16.6.561.22141.

Weierich, M.R. and Nock, M.K. (2008). Posttraumatic stress symptoms mediate the relation between childhood sexual abuse and nonsuicidal self-injury. *Journal of Consulting and Clinical Psychology*, 76(1), 39–44.

WHO. (2007). *Preventing Suicide in Jails and Prisons*. Geneva: World Health Organisation.

Wichmann, C., Serin, R. and Abracen, J. (2002). *Women Offenders Who Engage in Self-Harm: A Comparative Investigation*. Ottawa, ON: Correctional Service Canada.

Wilkins, J. and Coid, J. (1991). Self-mutilation in female remanded prisoners: I. An indicator of severe psychopathy. *Criminal Behaviour and Mental Health*, 1: 247–267.

Wilson, D. (2005). *Death at the Hands of the State*. London: Howard League for Penal Reform.

Wolf, A., Silva, F., Knight, K., and Javdani, S. (2007). Responding to the health needs of female offenders. In Rosemary Sheelan, editor. *What Works with Women Offenders*. Devon: Willan Publishing.

Wool, R. and Dooley, E. (1987). A study of attempted suicides in prisons. *Medicine, Science and the Law*, 27 (4), 297–301.

Women's Aid (2011). *Supporting Women Offenders Who Have Experienced Domestic and Sexual Violence*. London: Women's Aid Publishing.

Women in Prison (2009). *Response to Together We Can End Violence Against Women*. London: Women in Prison.

Women and Young People's Team (2010). *Supporting Women Affected By Violence: Guidelines for Staff*. London: Ministry of Justice.

Worden, J. W. (2003). *Grief Counselling and Grief Therapy: A Handbook for the Mental Health Practitioner*. London: Routledge.

Wright, L., Borrill, J., Teers, R. and Cassidy, T. (2006). The mental health consequences of dealing with self-inflicted death in custody. *Counselling Psychology Quarterly*, 19(2), 165–180.

Young, M.H., Justice, J. V., and Erdberg, P. (2006). Risk of harm: Inmates who harm themselves while in prison psychiatric treatment. *Journal of Forensic Science*, 51(1), 156–162.

Zlotnick, C., Mattia, J.I., and Zimmerman, M. (1999). Clinical correlates of self-mutilation in a sample of general psychiatric patients. *Journal of Nervous and Mental Disorders*, 187, 296–301.

Index

juvenile detention facilities *135*

L

M

N

Cries For Help: Women Without a Voice, Women's Prisons in the 1970s, Myra Hindley and her Contemporaries
by Joanna Kozubska. With a Foreword by Lord David Ramsbotham.

Opens a window on the closed world of Holloway, other women's prisons and the lives of those held there in the 1970s. This was an era when personal style and charismatic leadership was the order of the day for governors and prison officers, before ideas of 'new management', when problems were solved using personal initiatives.

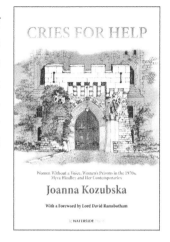

Paperback & Ebook | ISBN 978-1-909976-05-4

2014 | 208 pages

Mothering Justice: Working with Mothers in Criminal and Social Justice Settings
Edited by Lucy Baldwin. With a Foreword by Vicky Pryce.

Written by experts with first-hand experience, Mothering Justice is the first whole book to take motherhood as a focus for criminal and social justice interventions. Covering the spectrum of interventions it also makes a powerful case that in particular the imprisonment of mothers and its effect on their children is unnecessary, unjust, devastating and wasteful.

Paperback & Ebook | ISBN 978-1-909976-23-8

2015 | 320 pages

www.WatersidePress.co.uk